Modern Critical Views

Chinua Achebe
Henry Adams
Aeschylus
S. Y. Agnon
Edward Albee
Raphael Alberti
Louisa May Alcott
A. R. Ammons
Sherwood Anderson
Aristophanes
Matthew Arnold
Antonin Artaud
John Ashbery
Margaret Atwood
W. H. Auden
Jane Austen
Isaac Babel
Sir Francis Bacon
James Baldwin
Honoré de Balzac
John Barth
Donald Barthelme
Charles Baudelaire
Simone de Beauvoir
Samuel Beckett
Saul Bellow
Thomas Berger
John Berryman
The Bible
Elizabeth Bishop
William Blake
Giovanni Boccaccio
Heinrich Böll
Jorge Luis Borges
Elizabeth Bowen
Bertolt Brecht
The Brontës
Charles Brockden Brown
Sterling Brown
Robert Browning
Martin Buber
John Bunyan
Anthony Burgess
Kenneth Burke
Robert Burns
William Burroughs
George Gordon, Lord
  Byron
Pedro Calderón de la Barca
Italo Calvino
Albert Camus
Canadian Poetry: Modern
  and Contemporary
Canadian Poetry through
  E. J. Pratt
Thomas Carlyle
Alejo Carpentier
Lewis Carroll
Willa Cather
Louis-Ferdinand Céline
Miguel de Cervantes

Geoffrey Chaucer
John Cheever
Anton Chekhov
Kate Chopin
Chrétien de Troyes
Agatha Christie
Samuel Taylor Coleridge
Colette
William Congreve & the
  Restoration Dramatists
Joseph Conrad
Contemporary Poets
James Fenimore Cooper
Pierre Corneille
Julio Cortázar
Hart Crane
Stephen Crane
e. e. cummings
Dante
Robertson Davies
Daniel Defoe
Philip K. Dick
Charles Dickens
James Dickey
Emily Dickinson
Denis Diderot
Isak Dinesen
E. L. Doctorow
John Donne & the
  Seventeenth-Century
  Metaphysical Poets
John Dos Passos
Fyodor Dostoevsky
Frederick Douglass
Theodore Dreiser
John Dryden
W, E. B. Du Bois
Lawrence Durrell
George Eliot
T. S. Eliot
Elizabethan Dramatists
Ralph Ellison
Ralph Waldo Emerson
Euripides
William Faulkner
Henry Fielding
F. Scott Fitzgerald
Gustave Flaubert
E. M. Forster
John Fowles
Sigmund Freud
Robert Frost
Northrop Frye
Carlos Fuentes
William Gaddis
Federico García Lorca
Gabriel García Márquez
André Gide
W. S. Gilbert
Allen Ginsberg
J. W. von Goethe

Nikolai Gogol
William Golding
Oliver Goldsmith
Mary Gordon
Günther Grass
Robert Graves
Graham Greene
Thomas Hardy
Nathaniel Hawthorne
William Hazlitt
H. D.
Seamus Heaney
Lillian Hellman
Ernest Hemingway
Hermann Hesse
Geoffrey Hill
Friedrich Hölderlin
Homer
A. D. Hope
Gerard Manley Hopkins
Horace
A. E. Housman
William Dean Howells
Langston Hughes
Ted Hughes
Victor Hugo
Zora Neale Hurston
Aldous Huxley
Henrik Ibsen
Eugène Ionesco
Washington Irving
Henry James
Dr. Samuel Johnson and
  James Boswell
Ben Jonson
James Joyce
Carl Gustav Jung
Franz Kafka
Yasonari Kawabata
John Keats
Søren Kierkegaard
Rudyard Kipling
Melanie Klein
Heinrich von Kleist
Philip Larkin
D. H. Lawrence
John le Carré
Ursula K. Le Guin
Giacomo Leopardi
Doris Lessing
Sinclair Lewis
Jack London
Robert Lowell
Malcolm Lowry
Carson McCullers
Norman Mailer
Bernard Malamud
Stéphane Mallarmé
Sir Thomas Malory
André Malraux
Thomas Mann

Modern Critical Views

Modern Critical Views

JAMES BALDWIN

Edited and with an introduction by

Harold Bloom
Sterling Professor of the Humanities
Yale University

CHELSEA HOUSE PUBLISHERS
New York ◊ Philadelphia

Library of Congress Cataloging-in-Publication Data
Main entry under title:
James Baldwin.

  (Modern critical views)
  Bibliography: p.
  Includes index.
  Summary: A collection of critical essays on Baldwin
and his works. Also includes a chronology of events in
the author's life.
  1. Baldwin, James, 1924–   – Criticism and
interpretation. [1. Baldwin, James, 1924–   – Criticism
and interpretation. 2. American literature –
History and criticism] I. Bloom, Harold. II. Series.
PS3552.A45Z72   1986   818'.5409   86-8238
ISBN 0-87754-708-4

Contents

Editor's Note

This volume gathers together what its editor considers to be the most useful criticism yet devoted to the writings of James Baldwin, reprinted here in the chronological order of its original publication. I am indebted to Henry Finder and Susan Laity for their invaluable assistance in researching and editing this book.

The editor's introduction analyzes Baldwin's rhetorical stance in his nonfictional prose, which I take to be his major achievement, both morally and aesthetically. F. W. Dupee begins the chronological sequence of criticism with his tribute to Baldwin as a polemical essayist, a tribute severely qualified by his awareness that: "When Baldwin replaces criticism with prophecy, he manifestly weakens his grasp of his role, his style, and his great theme itself." In a related critique, Marcus Klein notes Baldwin's "rhetoric of privileged alienation," which sorts oddly with fictions whose heroes are always pre-moral, as it were.

In an astute review of Baldwin's play *Blues for Mr. Charlie*, the novelist Philip Roth grimly observes that making a hero of blackness, and sentimentalizing masculinity, are not in themselves sufficient to create drama. Considering *Another Country*, Charles Newman discovers Baldwin's precursor not in Richard Wright, but in Henry James. Dangerous as the comparison was, Newman intended it as a tribute to the potential revealed by *Another Country*, but twenty years later we have to read Newman with a certain melancholy nostalgia, since *Another Country* is unmatched by Baldwin's later fictions.

In another essay that contextualizes Baldwin, this time in the Church of his origins, Edward Margolies broods on the problematics of Baldwin's rage, with its perpetual capacity to flood both his novels and his essays. Roger Rosenblatt, in an analysis of *Go Tell It on the Mountain* and *Another Country*, traces how intricately sexuality and faith are interlaced throughout Baldwin's early novels.

A constant polemic against Baldwin, to the effect that he is far too contaminated by Western culture to be a true champion of the Black literature of liberation, is reflected in Marion Berghahn's survey of the images of Africa in Baldwin's writings. Pearl K. Bell, comparing Baldwin's difficulties with blacks to Philip Roth's parallel agon with Jewish critics, sadly concludes that *Just Above My Head* fails as a novel precisely because Baldwin has so uncertain a relation to his own people.

The British critic C. W. E. Bigsby, in a dispassionate overview of all of Baldwin's work, decides that the novelist-essayist's divided sensibility is finally his catastrophe, since his terrible ambivalences are never resolved by any intellectual synthesis. One aspect of those ambivalences is discussed by Stephen Adams, who considers *Giovanni's Room* as a lament for the unrealized possibilities of homosexual love, while it nevertheless seeks to present the homosexual as hero.

In a final estimate of Baldwin, James Snead reviews *The Price of the Ticket* and *The Evidence of Things Not Seen*, and honors the author as the most prolific and most durable American essayist of the last forty years. Snead's moving and careful tribute returns this volume full-circle to its editor's introduction, where the strengths and the opacities of Baldwin's essays are balanced against one another.

Introduction

I

Whatever the ultimate canonical judgment upon James Baldwin's fiction may prove to be, his nonfictional work clearly has permanent status in American literature. Baldwin seems to me the most considerable moral essayist now writing in the United States, and is comparable to George Orwell as a prose Protestant in stance. The evangelical heritage never has abandoned the author of *Go Tell It on the Mountain*, and Baldwin, like so many American essayists since Emerson, possesses the fervor of a preacher. Unlike Emerson, Baldwin lacks the luxury of detachment, since he speaks, not for a displaced Yankee majority, but for a sexual minority within a racial minority, indeed for an aesthetic minority among black homosexuals.

Ultimately, Baldwin's dilemma as a writer compelled to address social torments and injustices is that he is a minority of one, a solitary voice breaking forth against himself (and all others) from within himself. Like Carlyle (and a single aspect of the perspectivizing Nietzsche), Baldwin is of the authentic lineage of Jeremiah, most inward of prophets. What Baldwin opposes is what might be called, in Jeremiah's language, the injustice of outwardness, which means that Baldwin always must protest, even in the rather unlikely event that his country ever were to turn from selfishness and cruelty to justice and compassion in confronting its underclass of the exploited poor, whether blacks, Hispanics, or others cast out by the Reagan Revolution.

It seems accurate to observe that we remember Jeremiah, unlike Amos or Micah, for his individuation of his own suffering, rather than for his social vision, such as it was. Baldwin might prefer to have been an Amos or a Micah, forerunners of Isaiah, rather than a Jeremiah, but like Jeremiah he is vivid as a rhetorician of his own psychic anguish and perplexities, and most memorable as a visionary of a certain involuntary isolation, an election that requires a dreadful cost of confirmation. As Baldwin puts it, the price of the ticket is to accept the real reasons for the human journey:

The price the white American paid for his ticket was to become white —: and, in the main, nothing more than that, or, as he was to insist, nothing less. This incredibly limited not to say dimwitted ambition has choked many a human being to death here: and this, I contend, is because the white American has never accepted the real reasons for his journey. I know very well that my ancestors had no desire to come to this place: but neither did the ancestors of the people who became white and who require of my captivity a song. They require of me a song less to celebrate my captivity than to justify their own.

The Biblical text that Baldwin alludes to here, Psalm 137, does begin with the song of the exiles from Zion ("and they that wasted us required of us mirth") but ends with a ferocious prophecy against the wasters, ourselves. No writer — black or white — warns us so urgently of "the fire next time" as Baldwin and Jeremiah do, but I hear always in both prophets the terrible pathos of origins:

Then the word of the Lord came unto me, saying,

Before I formed thee in the belly I knew thee; and before thou camest forth out of the womb I sanctified thee, and I ordained thee a prophet unto the nations.

Then said I, Ah, Lord God! behold, I cannot speak: for I am a child.

We: my family, the living and the dead, and the children coming along behind us. This was a complex matter, for I was not living with my family in Harlem, after all, but "down-town," in the "white world," in alien and mainly hostile territory. On the other hand, for me, then, Harlem was almost as alien and in a yet more intimidating way and risked being equally hostile, although for very different reasons. This truth cost me something in guilt and confusion, but it was the truth. It had something to do with my being the son of an evangelist and having been a child evangelist, but this is not all there was to it — that is, guilt is not all there was to it.

The fact that this particular child had been born when and where he was born had dictated certain expectations. The child does not really know what these expectations are — does not know how real they are — until he begins to fail, challenge, or defeat them. When it was clear, for example, that the pulpit, where I had made so promising a beginning, would not be my career, it was hoped that

I would go on to college. This was never a very realistic hope and—perhaps because I knew this—I don't seem to have felt very strongly about it. In any case, this hope was dashed by the death of my father.

Once I had left the pulpit, I had abandoned or betrayed my role in the community—indeed, my departure from the pulpit and my leaving home were almost simultaneous. (I had abandoned the ministry in order not to betray myself by betraying the ministry.)

Reluctant prophets are in the position of Jonah; they provide texts for the Day of Atonement. Baldwin is always at work reexamining everything, doing his first works over; as he says: "Sing or shout or testify or keep it to yourself: but *know whence you came.*" We came crying hither because we came to this great stage of fools, but Baldwin, like Jeremiah and unlike Shakespeare, demands a theology of origins. He finds it in self-hatred, which he rightly insists is universal, though he seems to reject or just not be interested in the Freudian account of our moral masochism, our need for punishment. The evangelical sense of conscious sin remains strong in Baldwin. Yet, as a moral essayist, he is post-Christian, and persuades us that his prophetic stance is not so much religious as aesthetic. A kind of aesthetic of the moral life governs his vision, even in the turbulence of *The Fire Next Time* and *No Name in the Street*, and helps make them his finest achievements so far.

II

The center of Baldwin's prophecy can be located in one long, powerful paragraph of *The Fire Next Time*:

"The white man's Heaven," sings a Black Muslim minister, "is the black man's Hell." One may object—possibly—that this puts the matter somewhat too simply, but the song is true, and it has been true for as long as white men have ruled the world. The Africans put it another way: When the white man came to Africa, the white man had the Bible and the African had the land, but now it is the white man who is being, reluctantly and bloodily, separated from the land, and the African who is still attempting to digest or to vomit up the Bible. The struggle, therefore, that now begins in the world is extremely complex, involving the historical role of Christianity in the realm of power—that is, politics—and in the realm of morals. In the realm of power, Christianity has operated with an unmitigated arrogance and cruelty—necessarily, since a religion ordinarily imposes on those who have discovered the true faith the spiritual duty of liberating the infidels. This particular true faith, moreover, is more deeply concerned about the soul than it is about the body, to which fact the flesh (and the corpses) of countless infidels bears witness. It goes without saying, then, that whoever questions the authority of the true faith also contests the right of the nations that hold this faith to rule over him — contests, in short, their title to his land. The spreading of the Gospel, regardless of the motives or the integrity or the heroism of some of the missionaries, was an absolutely indispensable justification for the planting of the flag. Priests and nuns and schoolteachers helped to protect and sanctify the power that was so ruthlessly being used by people who were indeed seeking a city, but not one in the heavens, and one to be made, very definitely, by captive hands. The Christian church itself — again, as distinguished from some of its ministers — sanctified and rejoiced in the conquests of the flag, and encouraged, if it did not formulate, the belief that conquest, with the resulting relative well-being of the Western populations, was proof of the favor of God. God had come a long way from the desert — but then so had Allah, though in a very different direction. God, going north, and rising on the wings of power, had become white, and Allah, out of power, and on the dark side of Heaven, had become — for all practical purposes, anyway — black. Thus, in the realm of morals the role of Christianity has been, at best, ambivalent. Even leaving out of account the remarkable arrogance that assumed that the ways and morals of others were inferior to those of Christians, and that they therefore had every right, and could use any means, to change them, the collision between cultures — and the schizophrenia in the mind of Christendom — had rendered the domain of morals as chartless as the sea once was, and as treacherous as the sea still is. It is not too much to say that whoever wishes to become a truly moral human being (and let us not ask whether or not this is possible; I think we must *believe* that it is possible) must first divorce himself from all the prohibitions, crimes, and hypocrisies of the Christian church. If the concept of God has any validity or any use, it can only be to make us larger, freer, and more loving. If God cannot do this, then it is time we got rid of Him.

This superb instance of Baldwin's stance and style as a moral essayist depends for its rhetorical power upon a judicious blend of excess and restraint. Its crucial sentence achieves prophetic authority:

It is not too much to say that whoever wishes to become a truly moral human being (and let us not ask whether or not this is possible; I think we must *believe* that it is possible) must first divorce himself from all the prohibitions, crimes, and hypocrisies of the Christian church.

The parenthesis, nobly skeptical, is the trope of a master rhetorician, and placing "believe" in italics nicely puts into question the problematics of faith. "Divorce," denounced by St. Paul as having been introduced because of our hardness of hearts, acquires the antithetical aura of the Church itself, while Christian prohibitions are assimilated (rather wickedly) to Christian crimes and hypocrisies. This is, rhetorically considered, good, unclean fun, but the burden is savage, and steeped in moral high seriousness. The strength of *The Fire Next Time* comes to rest in its final paragraph, with the interplay between two italicized rhetorical questions, an interplay kindled when "*then*" is added to the second question:

When I was very young, and was dealing with my buddies in those wine- and urine-stained hallways, something in me wondered, *What will happen to all that beauty?* For black people, though I am aware that some of us, black and white, do not know it yet, are very beautiful. And when I sat at Elijah's table and watched the baby, the women, and the men, and we talked about God's — or Allah's — vengeance, I wondered, when that vengeance was achieved, *What will happen to all that beauty then?* I could also see that the intransigence and ignorance of the white world might make that vengeance inevitable — a vengeance that does not really depend on, and cannot really be executed by, any person or organization, and that cannot be prevented by any police force or army: historical vengeance, a cosmic vengeance, based on the law that we recognize when we say, "Whatever goes up must come down." And here we are, at the center of the arc, trapped in the gaudiest, most valuable, and most improbable water wheel the world has ever seen. Everything now, we must assume, is in our hands; we have no right to assume otherwise. If we — and now I mean the relatively conscious whites and the relatively conscious blacks, who must, like lovers, insist on, or create, the consciousness of the others — do not falter in our duty now, we may be able, handful that we are, to end the racial nightmare, and achieve our country, and change the history of the world. If we do not now dare everything, the fulfillment of that prophecy, recreated from the Bible in song by a slave, is upon us: "God gave Noah the rainbow sign, No more water, the fire next time!"

The shrewd rhetorical movement here is from the waterwheel to the ambivalent divine promise of no second flood, the promise of covenant with its dialectical countersong of the conflagration ensuing from our violation of covenant. That vision of impending fire re-illuminates the poignant question: "*What will happen to all that beauty then?*" All that beauty that is in jeopardy transcends even the beauty of black people, and extends to everything human, and to bird, beast, and flower.

No Name in the Street takes its fierce title from Job 18:16–19, where it is spoken to Job by Bildad the Shuhite, concerning the fate of the wicked:

> His roots shall be dried up beneath,
> and above shall his branch be cut off.
> His remembrance shall perish from the earth,
> and he shall have no name in the street.
> He shall be driven from light into darkness,
> and chased out of the world.
> He shall neither have son nor nephew among
> his people, nor any remaining in his dwellings.
> They that come after him shall be astonied
> at his day, as they that went before were
> affrighted.

I have to admit, having just read (and re-read) my way through the 690 pages of *The Price of the Ticket*, that frequently I am tempted to reply to Baldwin with Job's response to Bildad:

> How long will ye vex my soul, and break me in
> pieces with words?
> These ten times have ye reproached me: ye are
> not ashamed that ye make yourselves strange to me.
> And be it indeed that I have erred, mine
> error remaineth with myself.
> If indeed ye will magnify yourselves against
> me, and plead against me my reproach.

Baldwin's rhetorical authority as prophet would be seriously impaired if he were merely a Job's comforter, Bildad rather than Jeremiah. *No Name in the Street* cunningly evades the risk that Baldwin will magnify himself against the reader, partly by the book's adroitness at stationing the author himself in the vulnerable contexts of his own existence, both in New York and in Paris. By not allowing himself (or his readers) to forget how perpetually a black homosexual aesthete and moralist, writer and preacher, must fight for his life, Baldwin earns the pathos of the prophetic predicament:

> I made such motions as I could to understand what was happening, and to keep myself afloat. But I had been away too long. It was not only that I *could* not readjust myself to life in New York—it was also that I *would* not: I was never going to be anybody's nigger again. But I was now to discover that the world has more than one way of keeping you a nigger, has evolved more than one way of skinning the cat; if the hand slips here, it tightens there, and now I was offered, gracefully indeed: membership in the club. I had lunch at some elegant bistros, dinner at some exclusive clubs. I tried to be understanding about my countrymen's concern for difficult me, and unruly mine—and I really *was* trying to be understanding, though not without some bewilderment, and, eventually, some malice. I began to be profoundly uncomfortable. It was a strange kind of discomfort, a terrified apprehension that I had lost my bearings. I did not altogether understand what I was hearing. I did not trust what I heard myself saying. In very little that I heard did I hear anything that reflected anything which *I* knew, or had endured, of life. My mother and my father, my brothers and my sisters were not present at the tables at which I sat down, and no one in the company had ever heard of them. My own beginnings, or instincts, began to shift as nervously as the cigarette smoke that wavered around my head. I was not trying to hold on to my wretchedness. On the contrary, if my poverty was coming, at last, to an end, so much the better, and it wasn't happening a moment too soon—and yet, I felt an increasing chill, as though the rest of my life would have to be lived in silence.

The discomfort of having lost bearings is itself a prophetic trope, and comes to its fruition in the book's searing final paragraph:

> To be an Afro-American, or an American black, is to be in the situation, intolerably exaggerated, of all those who have ever found themselves part of a civilization which they could in no wise honorably defend—which they were compelled, indeed, endlessly to attack and condemn—and who yet spoke out of the most passionate love, hoping to make the kingdom new, to make it

honorable and worthy of life. Whoever is part of whatever civilization helplessly loves some aspects of it, and some of the people in it. A person does not lightly elect to oppose his society. One would much rather be at home among one's compatriots than be mocked and detested by them. And there is a level on which the mockery of the people, even their hatred, is moving because it is so blind: it is terrible to watch people cling to their captivity and insist on their own destruction. I think black people have always felt this about America, and Americans, and have always seen, spinning above the thoughtless American head, the shape of the wrath to come.

Not to be at home among one's compatriots is to avoid the catastrophe of being at ease in the new Zion that is America. A reader, however moved by Baldwin's rhetorical authority, can be disturbed here by the implication that all blacks are prophets, at least in our society. Would to God indeed that all the Lord's people were prophets, but they are not, and cannot be. Fourteen years after the original publication of *No Name in the Street*, I am confronted by polls indicating that the President of the United States, currently enjoying a sixty-eight percent approval rating among all his constituents, also possesses a rather surprising fifty percent endorsement from my black fellow citizens. Whatever the President's place in history may prove to be, time has darkened Baldwin's temporal prophecy that his own people could remain an undivided witness against our civilization.

III

Like every true prophet, Baldwin passionately would prefer the fate of Jonah to that of Jeremiah, but I do not doubt that his authentic descent from Jeremiah will continue to be valid until the end of his life (and mine). The final utterance in *The Price of the Ticket* seems to me Baldwin's most poignant, ever:

> Freaks are called freaks and are treated as they are treated—in the main, abominably—because they are human beings who cause to echo, deep within us, our most profound terrors and desires.
>
> Most of us, however, do not appear to be freaks—though we are rarely what we appear to be. We are, for the most part, visibly male or female, our social roles defined by our sexual equipment.
>
> But we are all androgynous, not only because we are all born of a woman impregnated by the seed of a man but because each

of us, helplessly and forever, contains the other—male in female, female in male, white in black and black in white. We are a part of each other. Many of my countrymen appear to find this fact exceedingly inconvenient and even unfair, and so, very often, do I. But none of us can do anything about it.

Baldwin is most prophetic, and most persuasive, when his voice is as subdued as it is here. What gives the rhetorical effect of self-subdual is the precise use of plural pronouns throughout. Moving from his own predicament to the universal, the prophet achieves an effect directly counter to Jeremiah's pervasive trope of individualizing the prophetic alternative. The ultimate tribute that Baldwin has earned is his authentic share in Jeremiah's most terrible utterance:

O Lord, thou has deceived me, and I was deceived: thou art stronger than I, and hast prevailed: I am in derision daily, every one mocketh me.

For since I spake, I cried out, I cried violence and spoil; because the word of the Lord was made a reproach unto me, and a derision, daily.

Then I said, I will not make mention of him, nor speak any more in his name. But his word was in mine heart as a burning fire shut up in my bones, and I was weary with forbearing, and I could not stay.

F. W. D U P E E

James Baldwin and "The Man"

As a writer of polemical essays on the Negro question James Baldwin has
no equals. He probably has, in fact, no real competitors. The literary role he
has taken on so deliberately and played with so agile an intelligence is one
that no white writer could possibly imitate and that few Negroes, I imagine,
would wish to embrace as a whole. Mr. Baldwin is the Negro *in extremis*, a
virtuoso of ethnic suffering, defiance and aspiration. His role is that of the
man whose complexion constitutes his fate, and not only in a society poisoned
by prejudice but, it sometimes seems, in general. For he appears to have received
a heavy dose of existentialism; he is at least half-inclined to see the Negro question
in the light of the Human Condition. So he wears his color as Hester Prynne
did her scarlet letter, proudly. And like her he converts this thing, in itself
so absurdly material, into a form of consciousness, a condition of spirit. Believing
himself to have been branded as different from and inferior to the white majority,
he will make a virtue of his situation. He will *be* different and in his own way
be better.

His major essays—for example, those collected in *Notes of a Native Son*—
show the extent to which he is able to be different and in his own way better.
Most of them were written, as other such pieces generally are, for the magazines,
some obviously on assignment. And their subjects—a book, a person, a locale,
an encounter—are the inevitable subjects of magazine essays. But Mr. Baldwin's
way with them is far from inevitable. To apply criticism "in depth" to *Uncle
Tom's Cabin* is, for him, to illuminate not only a book, an author, an age,
but a whole strain in the country's culture. Similarly with those routine themes,

From *"The King of the Cats" and Other Remarks on Writers and Writing*, 2d ed. © 1971 by
the Estate of F. W. Dupee. The University of Chicago Press, 1984.

the Paris expatriate and Life With Father, which he treats in "Equal In Paris" and the title piece of *Notes of a Native Son*, and which he wholly transfigures. Of course the transfiguring process in Baldwin's essays owes something to the fact that the point of view is a Negro's, an outsider's, just as the satire of American manners in *Lolita* and *Morte d'Urban* depends on their being written from the angle of, respectively, a foreign-born creep and a Catholic priest of American birth. But Baldwin's point of view in his essays is not merely that of the generic Negro. It is, as I have said, that of a highly stylized Negro whose language is distinguished by clarity, brevity, and a certain formal elegance. He is in love with syntax, with sentences that mount through clearly articulated stages to a resounding and clarifying climax and then gracefully subside. For instance this one, from *The Fire Next Time*:

> Girls, only slightly older than I was, who sang in the choir or taught
> Sunday school, the children of holy parents, underwent, before my
> eyes, the incredible metamorphosis, of which the most bewildering
> aspect was not their budding breasts or their rounding behinds but
> something deeper and more subtle, in their eyes, their heat, their
> odor, and the inflection of their voices.

Nobody else in democratic America writes sentences quite like this anymore. They suggest the ideal prose of an ideal literary community, some aristocratic France of one's dreams. This former Harlem boy has undergone his own incredible metamorphosis.

His latest book, *The Fire Next Time*, differs in important ways from his earlier work in the essay. Its subjects are less concrete, less clearly defined; to a considerable extent he has exchanged criticism for prophecy, analysis for exhortation and the results for his mind and style are in part disturbing. *The Fire Next Time* gets its title from a slave song: "God gave Noah the rainbow sign,/No more water, the fire next time." But this small book with the incendiary title consists of two independent essays, both in the form of letters. One is a brief affair entitled "My Dungeon Shook" and addressed to "My Nephew on the One Hundredth Anniversary of the Emancipation." The ominous promise of this title is fulfilled in the text. Between the hundred-year-old anniversary and the fifteen-year-old nephew the disparity is too great even for a writer of Baldwin's rhetorical powers. The essay reads like some specimen of "public speech" as practiced by MacLeish or Norman Corwin. It is not good Baldwin.

The other, much longer, much more significant essay appeared first in a pre-Christmas number of *The New Yorker*, where it made, understandably, a sensation. It is called "Down At the Cross: Letter From a Region of My Mind." The subtitle should be noted. Evidently the essay is to be taken as only a partial or provisional declaration on Mr. Baldwin's part, a single piece of his mind. Much of it, however, requires no such appeal for caution on the reader's part. Much of it is unexceptionably first-rate. For example, the reminiscences of the writer's boyhood, which form the lengthy introduction. Other of Baldwin's writings have made us familiar with certain aspects of his Harlem past. Here he concentrates on quite different things: the boy's increasing awareness of the abysmally narrow world of choice he inhabits as a Negro, his attempt to escape a criminal existence by undergoing a religious conversion and becoming at fifteen a revivalist preacher, his discovery that he must learn to "inspire fear" if he hopes to survive the fear inspired in him by "the man"— the white man.

In these pages we come close to understanding why he eventually assumed his rather specialized literary role. It seems to have grown naturally out of his experience of New York City. As distinct from a rural or small-town Negro boy, who is early and firmly taught "his place," young Baldwin knew the treacherous fluidity and anonymity of the metropolis where hidden taboos and unpredictable animosities lay in wait for him and a trip to the 42nd Street Library could be a grim adventure. All this part of the book is perfect; and when Baldwin finally gets to what is his ostensible subject, the Black Muslims or Nation of Islam movement, he is very good too. As good, that is, as possible considering that his relations with the movement seem to have been slight. He once shared a television program with Malcolm X, "the movement's second-in-command," and he paid a brief and inconclusive visit to the first-in-command, the Honorable Elijah Muhammad and his entourage at the party's headquarters in Chicago. (Muhammad ranks as a prophet; to him the Black Muslim doctrines were "revealed by Allah Himself.") Baldwin reports the Chicago encounter in charming detail and with what looks like complete honesty. On his leaving the party's rather grand quarters, the leader insisted on providing him with a car and driver to protect him "from the white devils until he gets wherever it is he is going." Baldwin accepted, he tells us, adding wryly: "I was, in fact, going to have a drink with several white devils on the other side of town."

He offers some data on the Black Muslim movement, its aims and finances. But he did a minimum of homework here. Had he done more he might at least have provided a solid base for the speculative fireworks the book abounds in. To cope thoroughly with the fireworks in short space, or perhaps any space, seems impossible. Ideas shoot from the book's pages as the sparks fly upward, in bewildering quantity and at random. I don't mean that it is all fireworks. On the cruel paradoxes of the Negro's life, the failures of Christianity, the relations of Negro and Jew, Baldwin is superb. But a lot of damage is done to his argument by his indiscriminate raids on Freud, Lawrence, Sartre, Genet and other psychologists, metaphysicians and melodramatists. Still more damage is done by his refusal to draw on anyone so humble as Martin Luther King and his fellow-practitioners of nonviolent struggle.

For example: "White Americans do not believe in death, and this is why the darkness of my skin so intimidates them." But suppose one or two white Americans are *not* intimidated. Suppose someone coolly asks what it means to "believe in death." Again: "Do I really *want* to be integrated into a burning house?" Since you have no other, yes; and the better-disposed firemen will welcome your assistance. Again: "A vast amount of the energy that goes into what we call the Negro problem is produced by the white man's profound desire not to be judged by those who are not white." You exaggerate the white man's consciousness of the Negro. Again: "The real reason that nonviolence is considered to be a virtue in Negroes . . . is that white men do not want their lives, their self-image, or their property threatened." Of course they don't, especially their lives. Moreover, this imputing of "real reasons" for the behavior of entire populations is self-defeating, to put it mildly. One last quotation, this time a regular apocalypse:

> In order to survive as a human, moving, moral weight in the world, America and all the Western nations will be forced to re-examine themselves and release themselves from many things that are now taken to be sacred, and to discard nearly all the assumptions that have been used to justify their lives and their anguish and their crimes so long.

Since whole cultures have never been known to "discard nearly all their assumptions" and yet remain intact, this amounts to saying that any essential improvement in Negro-white relations, and thus in the quality of American life, is unlikely.

So much for the fireworks. What damage, as I called it, do they do to the writer and his cause—which is also the concern of plenty of others? When Baldwin replaces criticism with prophecy, he manifestly weakens his grasp of his role, his style, and his great theme itself. And to what end? Who is likely to be moved by such arguments, unless it is the more literate Black Muslims, whose program Baldwin specifically rejects as both vindictive and unworkable. And with the situation as it is in Mississippi and elsewhere—dangerous, that is, to the Negro struggle and the whole social order—is not a writer of Baldwin's standing obliged to submit his assertions to some kind of pragmatic test, some process whereby their truth or untruth will be gauged according to their social utility? He writes: "The Negroes of this country may never be able to rise to power, but they are very well placed indeed to precipitate chaos and ring down the curtain on the American dream." I should think that the anti-Negro extremists were even better placed than the Negroes to precipitate chaos, or at least to cause a lot of trouble; and it is unclear to me how *The Fire Next Time*, in its madder moments, can do anything except inflame the former and confuse the latter.

MARCUS KLEIN

A Question of Identity

The invisibility of the Negro in America has in fact been James Baldwin's underlying metaphor also, and when he has been most responsive to his materials he has made of invisibility, the failure of identity, a lyric of frustration and loss. What is most revealing for the case Baldwin comes to represent, however, is that the fury in his frustration and the pathos in his loss have led him, in a progress of three novels and far too many personal essays, ever further from the clarity with which he began. What promised to be a dramatic recognition of the actual conditions of invisibility in his first novel, *Go Tell It on the Mountain* (1953), became a rhetoric of privileged alienation. As a Negro, Baldwin was society's victim. As a victim, he was alienated. As an alienatee, he presented himself with vast moral authority. In the space of a few years the rhetoric and the authority have done him less and less service, and he has been left to fall back on an iteration of the word "love." Love in its demonstration has become, finally, a fantasy of innocence.

The plight in invisibility has remained a plight for Baldwin, despite his uses of it as an instrument of moral authority and despite the fury in his words. His heroes are victims, caught between despair and spite, their spitefulness directed sometimes against the very sympathy which as victims they earn. They are heroes who cannot make themselves felt in the world, heroes for whom society almost provides but then doesn't quite provide a clear, felt identity. The story Baldwin tells repeatedly, in his novels, his stories, his writing for the theater, and in his essays, is of the attempt of a heroic innocent to achieve what Baldwin usually calls "identity" – "identity" is by all measure his favorite

From *After Alienation: American Novels in Mid-Century.* © 1962, 1964 by The World Publishing Co. New York Books for Libraries Press, 1970. Originally entitled "James Baldwin: A Question of Identity."

word, but on occasion the word is "manhood" or "maturity"—and the thwarting, then, of this hero by his society. The hero is prevented from entering the world. He does not achieve the definition provided by a place in the world. If sometimes in a final movement he does locate himself in a peripheral place and in a special expression of the self, in the expatriate community of Paris, perhaps, or the world of jazz, more often he finds himself shunted into one or another expression of neurosis—religious mania in *Go Tell It on the Mountain* and in Baldwin's play *The Amen Corner*, homosexuality elsewhere, a nightmare violence such as that in the first movement of *Another Country* (1962). And the hero's fulfillment stands, then, ironically and bitterly, for the quantity of his pain.

The hero's plight in Baldwin's fiction and semifiction has many equivalences. To be a Negro in Harlem is, it turns out, the same thing really as to be an American Negro abroad. That, in turn, is the same thing as to be an upper-middle-class Negro in Atlanta, Georgia, or it is the same thing as to be a Northern Negro visiting in Atlanta. Given a slight shift of circumstances, to be an American Negro at all is the same thing as to be an American, and then to be an American is the same thing as to be sexually ambivalent. The adventures of Baldwin's different heroes have a sameness. An occasional essay in 1959 on school integration in Atlanta, "Nobody Knows My Name," discovers its principal interest in those middle-class Negroes of Atlanta who, because of their inherited position, cannot fully find themselves in either camp, white or black. There is the story, it would seem, that Baldwin is best equipped to see. And their condition is different only in what may be called accident from what would seem to be its opposite case, that of the hero of Baldwin's "white" novel, *Giovanni's Room* (1956), whose inherited condition is simply that he is an American. As an American, the novel argues, he cannot love, and therefore he cannot give himself to either camp of lovers, heterosexuals' or homosexuals'. In both instances the protagonists are born to a fatal ambivalence of position which confers on them a kind of invisibility. They suffer the same manifest nonexistence in society. And their story, once again, is not essentially different from that of the American Negro in Paris who is the subject of a number of Baldwin's essays, whose American-ness separates him from Europeans while his color does not allow him to be an American. He is separated by his nationality, moreover, from other colored persons, the North Africans in Paris, and he is separated by the motives of his expatriation from other American Negroes in Paris. The "American Negro in Paris," Baldwin indeed says in one of these essays, "Encounter on the Seine," "is very nearly the invisible man."

And it is the loneliness in invisibility that is the affective basis of this constant story. Baldwin's heroes are projected as having an original, unique identity, which society does not so much corrupt as obscure. "Nobody Knows

My Name" might stand as the title for everything that Baldwin has written—
as in fact it does stand as the title for his second collection of essays. The
yearning of all his heroes, in their many circumstances, is for recognition, and
they find themselves enmeshed in society's misunderstandings. In Ellison's use
of the metaphor, invisibility became the hero's essential identity—Rinehart,
the underground man, and the Invisible Man are citizens of the invisible world
which is the other side of this phenomenal world. Invisibility in Baldwin's use
of it is the cloak of unseeing which society forces upon the hero, which hides
his unchanged identity, and which imprisons him therefore in anonymity.

The matter is not entirely a simple one. Identity, Baldwin is to be found
saying often enough, is something to be *attained* or *achieved*, especially in America,
most especially by a Negro, and that is to imply that "identity" is dynamic
and progressive. The Negro's past, he says, is an "endless struggle *to achieve*
and reveal and confirm a human identity." And Baldwin says: "The necessity
of Americans *to achieve* an identity is a historical and a present personal fact. . . ."
Commenting on someone's incidental observation that the trouble with Norman
Mailer is that he is white, he says:

> What my friend meant was that to become a Negro man, let alone
> a Negro artist, *one had to make oneself up as one went along.* This
> had to be done in the not-at-all metaphorical teeth of the world's
> determination to destroy you. . . . This is not the way this truth
> presents itself to white men, who believe the world is theirs and
> who, albeit unconsciously, expect the world to help them in the
> achievement of their identity. But the world does not do this—for
> anyone.

Identity, that is to say, is created in experience and in the consequent yielding
of innocence. Or identity is merely maturity. And in his fiction, which of course
depends on some forward movement, Baldwin's hero struggles against the
invisibility that has been thrust upon him and he thereby does make an effort
to define himself.

But the *achievement* of identity isn't the story Baldwin actually tells. The
identity to be achieved, it always turns out, even when the effort is announced
as successful, is that identity that the hero has always had. It is his birthright,
which society had obscured from him. In a number of essays, for instance,
Baldwin has discussed his own expatriation to Paris in the years just after the
war, and the point of all these essays is that expatriation, while it confirmed
his invisibility, gave him opportunity, not to discover, but to recover himself.
So he says, "From the vantage point of Europe [the American student] discovers
his own country." In an atmosphere, Baldwin says, in which the racial matter

was relaxed, he found again both his American-ness and his Negro-ness. The American Negro discovers that his birthright is distinct from that of the African.

> I left America because I doubted my ability to survive the fury of the color problem here. . . . In my necessity to find the terms on which my experience could be related to that of others, Negroes and whites, writers and nonwriters, I proved, to my astonishment, to be as American as any Texas GI.

In other personal essays more or less concerned with identity, Baldwin's chief occupation is actually his own childhood. "Identity" is something that one once had, or at least almost had, in the past, in childhood. And indeed, the child who has not yet quite defined himself but who has not yet either been lost is, an inventory would prove, Baldwin's favorite subject.

The hero who is dispossessed of his place, robbed of his identity in the world, and who is therefore lonely, is everywhere in Baldwin's writing, where it is his story Baldwin sets out to tell and, more significantly, where it isn't. The hero of an occasional interview with Ingmar Bergman becomes, expressly, Baldwin himself. ". . . I amused myself, on the ride back into town, by projecting a movie. . . and it then occurred to me that my bitterness might be turned to good account if I should dare to envision the tragic hero for whom I was searching—as myself. All art is a kind of confession. . . . " And the vision to which the piece comes is, only not quite so expressly, of that hero who is lost in a society that does not confer definition. Bergman, in Stockholm, had his father, his past, and therefore a perception of moral authority on which to draw. Baldwin's New York is a place where youngsters were "searching desperately for the limits which would tell them who they were. . . . " There is something to impress loneliness even in the melancholy past tense in which the observation is cast. Again, an essay, "Faulkner and Desegregation" begins: "Any real change implies the breakup of the world as one has always known it, the loss of all that gave one an identity, the end of safety," and manages at a stroke to insert Faulkner into a drama of loneliness. Baldwin's response to the position Faulkner took on desegregation is, of course, indignation, but the device of Baldwin's indignation is—as it is elsewhere for Norman Mailer, then for the whole United States delegation to the United Nations, for white Americans generally and for Negroes generally—pity that one should be so lonely, so outside the world.

The recovery of identity is the theme, and the drama is in the hero's loneliness and the injustice of his having to strive for identity in the world that would make him invisible. The recovery of identity, it is suggested, will be the means of his accommodation in the world. But it has been Baldwin's difficulty as a novelist, briefly, that with the discovery of loneliness—enunciated sometimes as a wail, sometimes as a sigh, sometimes with a graceful bitterness, occasionally in radical obscenities—he has tended to end his explorations. There is no doubt that his hero suffers authentic affliction, an affliction that takes ingenious, complicated forms—and that, too, is something that Baldwin knows very well. "Complication" and its cognates, when he is describing his lack of identity, are words constantly at his lips. But still it is not the complicated affliction, despite his knowledge of it, not what it is to *be* an invisible man, but how and how much it hurts, the pity of it, that engages Baldwin.

Pity with some sarcasm in it has been the mode of his indignation, and pity without sarcasm has been the usual mode of the honor he pays to his heroes. Pity is his note, available both to his heroes and to his villains, who do occupy an identical position. They are all outside the world. They are pitiful because, being outside the world, they are unable to attain any normal social connection with it. That is the despair of invisibility. They are without parental love, if it is a child's story that Baldwin is telling, or they are without romantic love, if it is that kind of story. Or they are expatriates and therefore without community. Or, as in the case Baldwin made out of Faulkner, they may be trapped in the archaic past and therefore disbarred from the social connection of current politics.

That is to say nothing, of course, about the truth of Baldwin's perceptions, in his fiction or his essays, but to say something only about their pattern and their circumscription. It is one story that Baldwin tells, even in his many fictions which are presented in the form of essays. And it is clear enough that the story is his own. The matter is in fact the more clear in Baldwin's many informal essays. Whatever their ostensible subject, what is most prominent in them is the pronoun "I." And the pity in Baldwin's response, either without or with its trill of sarcasm, is finally, without exception, pity for himself.

To discover that his sorrow is self-centered is not, of course, to discover Baldwin in a breach of etiquette. A writer of fiction does write out of himself, and self-pity might be the means of his perception. All art is a kind of confession. The pity, when it is intensive, may be a device of analysis, the way into the detail of a particular reality.

Baldwin's uses of his pity for himself have been largely extensive and repetitive, and one of the results of *his* self-pity would seem to be that as a novelist he has made a specialty of the informal essay. One looks to the essays for the motives of the fiction. The essays are indeed always dramatic—they are passionate, a sentience moves through them. They do include real experience—Baldwin's own, but slightly transformed by their subjects. And they are "personal," in the sense not of coziness, but in the fact that they create a person. They are quite as much concerned with the style—the identity, precisely—of the man speaking as they are with their various topics. They have that feeling of an intimate involvement. They are themselves, that is to say, *almost* fiction.

But then they aren't fiction. One expects of serious fiction a thoroughness and a probing that Baldwin's essays have not, a progress of events, a moving through contradiction and complication. The pity Baldwin brings in his essays to what is at bottom always his own plight does not move. It is already completely formulated, and it is not analytic but appreciative. It stops short. Fiction pure would demand that he go on, into himself, that he participate in himself. And the informal essay permits him the pity without real involvement. It permits him to shift ground and in many various ways to repeat himself without going on to an end. The essays present him with many applications of an insight he has already had into his own nature and situation, and excuse him from the imaginative pursuit of it.

The essays don't have the seriousness of fiction. It happens, and by the same measure, that they don't have the seriousness of essays either, even though the insight on which they are built has every validity. The single insight does apply equally to Baldwin's own experience as a Negro and an American, and to what was the position of William Faulkner, and to that of expatriates in Paris, and, in fact, to everyone everywhere. Raised to its metaphysical dimensions, it is that insight into man's perpetual condition which tells of man's loneliness on this isthmus of a middle state. It is the insight which Baldwin latterly, with a flourish, has come to call the tragic sense of life. There is in it not only a truth, but a cliché which becomes a significant truth only when one gets down to cases. And Baldwin's difficulty as an essayist, briefly, is that he tends to arouse expectations of cases which he doesn't satisfy. If, by writing essays, he evades the demands of fiction, by writing essays as fiction he evades the demand of thorough ideas.

In the essays, he creates character, a series of images of himself. That is the chief function of his rhetoric, and the dramatic rhetoric not infrequently substitutes for substantial argument. Baldwin establishes an attitude toward issues, or he establishes a person in the act of confronting them, but on the one hand the person is not pursued and then on the other hand the issues themselves are left often unconfronted. There is a person in these essays always, one feels, about to make himself clear, about to say something that will be, because he is so involved, really illuminating—and then there is a rhetorical flourish and what "ideas" are produced, especially given the advertised engagement, are only flat or hopelessly vast.

An essay on the Negro Muslims concludes, for instance:

Any effort, from here on out, to keep the Negro in his "place" can only have the most extreme and unlucky repercussions. This being so, it would seem to me that the most intelligent effort we can now make is to give up this doomed endeavor and study how we can most quickly end this division in our house. The Negroes who rioted in the U.N. are but a very small echo of the black discontent now abroad in the world. If we are not able, and quickly, to face and begin to eliminate the sources of this discontent in our own country, we will never be able to do it on the great stage of the world.

Now this is all very strong, very stern, and it has lofty solemnity. Moreover, it is true. But in fact it doesn't quite come to the point of discourse. It is at best newsy—there is a new, more militant black discontent abroad in the world—but then that is at best stale news. The threat in the advice is of the evaporating sort, carefully modulated into pathos, and the advice in it is an instrument which frustrates talk about the issues—just how will we go about ending "this division in our house"? The essay sends the issues off, as it were, to committee. What the statement finally presents is *merely* drama. The statement creates a hero, Baldwin himself, who is being ominous and militant but goodwilled, too, and who is telling us for the last time. The hero is not so militant, it should be said, as the Muslim rioters who are Baldwin's subject—one might speculate on Baldwin's use here and in a number of other essays of "we." By taking the Muslims' case really as his own, he might not only make a political statement but he would commit a political act. There would be an idea in it, if not a reasonable one. He stops short of that, as he does in his later, more elaborate discussion of the Muslims in "Letter from a Region in My Mind." Both essays exist after all only to supply a hero with an attitude, to supply Baldwin with the dramatic component of an idea.

When Baldwin speaks on the current politics of the Negro's situation in America, what is ultimately accomplished is a prophetic posture, a hero threatening an apocalypse which is itself lacking in particulars. "Any honest examination of the national life," Baldwin says, "proves how far we are from the standard of human freedom with which we began. . . . If we are not capable of this examination, we may yet become one of the most distinguished and monumental failures in the history of nations." He says:

When a race riot occurs in Atlanta, it will not spread merely to Birmingham. . . . (Birmingham is a doomed city.) The trouble will spread to every metropolitan center in the nation which has a significant Negro population. And this is not only because the ties

between Northern and Southern Negroes are still very close. It is
because the nation, the entire nation, has spent a hundred years
avoiding the question of the place of the black man in it.

He says: "the white man's world, intellectually, morally, and spiritually, has
the meaningless ring of a hollow drum and the odor of slow death." It is all
true, of course. But the process by which the truth was to be dramatized,
given a human voice and a human action, has somehow become more important
than the truth. Where it should be, there is the author full of large eloquence.

In other moods Baldwin seizes subjects in order to project, it may be, a
role of besieged integrity, or perhaps of terribly calm paternity—the need of
the young for an image of authority provides Baldwin with a frequent
parenthesis. Or the role may be one of a lonely outsider who is really an insider.
So he pauses, for instance, in his essay on Norman Mailer, to say: ". . . the
things that most white people imagine that they can salvage from the storm
of life are really, in sum, their innocence. It was this commodity precisely which
I had to get rid of at once"; and then he says again, in reply to Mailer's
speculations on the nature of power, "Well, I know how power works, it has
worked on me, and if I didn't know how power worked, I would be dead."
The least observation to be made is that this essay on Mailer is about Baldwin.
Baldwin calls it "The Black Boy Looks at the White Boy," but in fact both
boys look for the most part at Baldwin. And the statement might be the
beginning of a deep narrative of what it is to be a Negro in the United States,
or it might be the credentials of a discursive idea, but the idea is not engaged,
and the statement after all is only an affective parenthesis, another flickering
view of the author in still another stance bespeaking loneliness and the unloved.

The affectation of ideas is bombast, and Baldwin's difficulty as an essayist
has been that he has allowed bombast to do his work. But then nothing proves
so clearly as this disappearance of ideas the nature of the frustrations he has
known as a novelist. The essays are almost without exception the statements
of a spokesman, of a Negro addressing whites. Spokesmanship is at least their
first intention. Baldwin *reports* as, naturally, a qualified insider, on such matters
as school integration in the South, anti-Semitism in Harlem, the Negro response
to American politicians, white and black. Spokesmanship, even for one who
is committed to it, must entail a first uncomfortable assumption that one is
speaking for a community, and that is an assumption that Baldwin particularly
must find difficult. He has at least once, in passing, in a review, said as much:
". . . popular belief to the contrary, it is not enough to have been born a Negro
to understand the history of Negroes in America." And Baldwin, whether or
not his representation is accepted, must find the assumption of spokesmanship

distressing because he is not committed to it, because his vision is personal. His subject is himself. And it is the evidence of his best work, in fiction and essays, that a spokesman is just what he does not want to be. Something like this reluctance must be behind the final equivocation of his essays that should be polemical, the strange use of a first-person plural that dissociates him from Negroes, the final failure to give his indignation the form and the force of argument.

Moreover, not only the lie, but the personal danger in spokesmanship, is something that Baldwin knows very well. He all but began his literary career, in an essay, "Everybody's Protest Novel," with a speculation on its dangers. The essay uses *Uncle Tom's Cabin* to define the hypocritical simplicities of protest literature. Mrs. Stowe's passions were sentimental, sociological, and theological, Baldwin says in effect, and she was therefore divorced by each of her passions from the complications of real human experience and real human beings. What she intended as salvation actually dehumanized. The great and subtle danger of her novel lies, however, not in its hot misguided liberalism, but in the acceptance by its victims of the terms of its dehumanization. For Baldwin, who was writing his own first novel as he wrote the essay, and clearly trying to define that novel, the seditious historical effect of *Uncle Tom's Cabin* was *Native Son*. "Bigger is Uncle Tom's descendant, flesh of his flesh, so exactly opposite a portrait that, when the books are placed together, it seems that the contemporary Negro novelist and the dead New England woman are locked together in a deadly, timeless battle. . . . " As a protest novel, *Native Son* accepts all of Mrs. Stowe's categorizing of tricksy, unique human identity, and it therefore creates a hero who "admits the possibility of his being subhuman" and who battles his world according to the criteria of an imposed black-white theology that has nothing to do with his humanity. "The failure of the protest novel lies in its rejection of life . . . in its insistence that it is [the human being's] categorization alone which is real and which cannot be transcended." And it follows therefore that the honest novelist will choose the uncategorized, individual human life.

This is really an easy enough, and in recent years it has been for everyone an obvious enough, thing to say. For Negro writers it has been obvious for a somewhat longer time, but harder. "What is today parroted," Baldwin says in the same essay, "as [the novelist's] Responsibility . . . is, when he believes it, his corruption and our loss," and it is clear that for Baldwin social responsibility was at the beginning of his career a clear and pressing problem. Because he was a Negro it must have been there waiting for him when he sat down to write. The fulfillment of such responsibility in any overt way, by protest or by spokesmanship, snuffs out all the complexity and the paradox of the individual human personality. Social responsibility is, too, the cloak of invisibility.

Then it would be the job of the novelist to be deliberately unmindful of his responsibility, to dive into the individual human personality, into the only one, presumably, the depths of which he can know, namely his own. The business of the novelist Baldwin in fact says, again in the same essay, is "revelation" of "the disquieting complexity of ourselves," "this web of ambiguity, paradox, this hunger, danger, darkness. . . ." And that elegant prescription is indeed implicit everywhere in Baldwin's writings. It is his advice to himself when he talks, as he does everywhere, of identity. And this conception of his task is not merely a choosing of the "psychological" or, perhaps, the "existential" novel over the "social" novel. For Baldwin certainly it has to do with the possibility of his writing honestly at all. That is a problem to which as a Negro writer he is simply born.

But for a Negro writer of talent and conscience there is no avoiding the burdens of spokesmanship, and it is not only a matter of conscience and of the obvious social necessities. Indeed, it would seem that for Baldwin the very attempt to avoid spokesmanship led him to it, and if he is not very good at it, that betrays not a failure of rigor or courage but a crisis of honesty. It is the fact that in all of his fictions, including his one "white" novel, writing honestly and in pursuit of the complex personal truth, he has found himself come around to the point where there is nothing else to do but howl his frustration, or turn to essays and write spokesmanlike protest. "It is quite impossible," Baldwin says in another early essay, "to write a worthwhile novel about a Jew or a Gentile or a Homosexual, for people refuse, unhappily, to function in so neat and one-dimensional a fashion." One can't, obviously, by the same token, write a novel about a Negro. But one can't either, Baldwin seems to have discovered repeatedly, write a story about a Negro and deny that he is a Negro, deny that what Ralph Ellison called the "little question of civil rights," what Alain Locke called the Negro's "shadow," do constitute much of the reality of the person.

That dilemma gives way to another. This Negro-ness as a personal reality may really be a kind of invisibility. The fact that he is a Negro, that his life is in great part the effect of a long history and a ramifying system of persecution, prevents what Baldwin calls identity. And so at the point of discovering Negro-ness, at the point where his heroes are about to discover it, Baldwin must turn to speak publicly as a Negro, to some immediately social purpose, therefore as a spokesman, to the distortion or abandonment of the personal identity. And then if he doesn't speak convincingly as a spokesman, it is because that personal identity, and not social salvation, was the goal.

The goal was the same, of course, for Ralph Ellison. A sense of the self was to be made compatible with a sense of society. In *Invisible Man* it is the pattern of frustrations that would seem to prevent identity that, ironically, creates it. The hero's invisibility becomes essential and positive. In Baldwin's fiction, the search for identity is, however, everywhere engaged in, and nowhere actually achieved, although there are instances when Baldwin would want us to believe it is achieved. His heroes are forever on their way to being something, or to being somebodies, when they find themselves suddenly in a labyrinthine confusion, identity denied them. And because identity isn't achieved—isn't, that is to say, identified—Baldwin's drama is finally the way identity is frustrated. His hero's climactic action, it follows, is suffering, and pity is Baldwin's comment.

But then something is attained, if only because in order to conceive that identity is the goal, Baldwin must contain in his drama some notion of what it would look like were it to be had. And what it would look like has as much to do with the fact that it cannot be attained as anything in the obvious public situation of the Negro. What is Baldwin's idea of identity is something that fiction in fact can't accomplish. It seems not only, in the case of his Negro heroes, to have nothing to do with Negro-ness, with color, but to be unrelated to any hair, bone, flesh, cartilage, circumstances, or experience. Its one identifiable, but not necessarily constant, component is sex. It is libido, or it is Soul, a small, pure, passionate flame. It is something always in the past. It is the sort of thing that life as seen in fiction must snuff out. Fiction is a gathering of experience in the world, and experience is what corrupts Baldwin's identity, and is its natural enemy.

Baldwin's idea of identity is after all, to use his own word, "theological"—and after all it would seem to make some difference, despite his intentions and his removal, that he was, as he has said, "practically born in the church." Richard Wright's Bigger Thomas suffers, Baldwin says, by his acceptance of the raging puritanical theology that moved Harriet Beecher Stowe—black is evil. But it is Baldwin himself who accepts what is a preliminary idea behind Mrs. Stowe's puritanism, that to be in the world at all is to be depraved. In the same essay Baldwin advises that "our humanity is our burden, our life; we need not battle for it; we need only to do what is infinitely more difficult—that is, accept it"—but that, the accepting of our humanity, is just what he makes it impossible for his heroes to do. The advice is not for Baldwin, what it might seem, merely a lofty glibness. It proposes the riddle within which his own fiction moves. Our humanity, if that means an involvement with our actions, is that which pollutes the pure expression of pure passion, and purity is what finally Baldwin seems to mean by identity.

A passion so pure that it is beyond all metaphors would seem to be Baldwin's idea ultimately of identity and reality. But only ultimately. In various places in his work—although not, it happens, in any chronological sequence of change—identity wears various guises, which look like identifications, the name that nobody knows. But then either the guises are not sustained, and what appeared to be identity is revealed to be only an attitude or a passing polemical opportunism, or the mask slips, or the mask fails because it is obviously not a face.

The Negro's and Baldwin's basic identity may reside, for instance, in the fact that Negroes are Americans. Americanism is one of Baldwin's guises. "Negroes are Americans," he says, "and their destiny is the country's destiny." The Negro "is not a visitor to the West, but a citizen there, an American; as American as the Americans who despise him, the Americans who fear him, the Americans who love him. . . . " The Negro "has been formed by this nation, for better or for worse, and does not belong to any other—not to Africa, and certainly not to Islam." In Europe the American Negro begins to realize his relationship to white Americans. "Now he is bone of their bone, flesh of their flesh; they have loved and hated and obsessed and feared each other and his blood is in their soil." These are of course statements of political implication, existing in a context where black nationalism, the quantity of the American Negro's alienation from America, is the question. But they also say what they say, that the American Negro is to be identified as American.

And that consideration might be for Baldwin the beginning of another, harder, more experiential idea of what identity is, but in fact it is only the beginning of an infinite regress because identity, Baldwin is to be found saying just as frequently, is just what Americans themselves don't have. The Negro identity may be that he is an American, but the American identity is nothing, or nothing yet that one can put one's finger on.

> America's history, her aspirations, her peculiar triumphs, her even more peculiar defeats, and her position in the world—yesterday and today—are all so profoundly and stubbornly unique that the very word "America" remains a new, almost completely undefined and extremely controversial proper noun. No one in the world seems to know exactly what it describes, not even we motley millions who call ourselves Americans.

The key words in the passage promise to be "almost" and "exactly"—if America is *almost* undefined and no one knows *exactly* what the name means, then one will expect that the author, especially as he is writing an essay called "The Discovery of What It Means to Be an American," will clarify the matter *somewhat*. But the passage says quite as much about what it is to be an American as the essay is going to say. America lacks definition. And elsewhere Baldwin speaks of the alienation of Americans from their own past and their inability therefore to know who they are, and he speaks elsewhere again of the American "confusion" and the American "incoherence." And then all arguments disappear when Baldwin speculates that it is lack of identity that makes Negroes American: "The necessity of Americans to achieve an identity is a historical and a present personal fact and this is the connection between you and me."

Just what it is that Americans, as such, don't have and that would fill them with identity, Baldwin suggests most particularly in *Giovanni's Room*. It seems to be sex. But prior to and beyond that discovery there are other guises of identity. In the single most searching, least equivocating essay Baldwin has written, the Negro's identity emerges from the cauldron of Western experience as Satanic. The essay, called "Stranger in the Village," begins with the event of Baldwin's brief residence in a tiny Swiss village where no black man before him had ever set foot, and from that pure case develops the drama of the Negro's basic estrangement in the West. It goes on to his citizenship in America, to make the point that the American racial drama is changing the culture of the West, but meanwhile, in the Swiss village and prior to the alteration of our culture, the Negro is given identity by Christian myth. The cathedral at Chartres says something to the villagers, or would say something to them if they could hear it, Baldwin says, that it does not say to him, but on the other hand it speaks to him as it cannot to them.

> Perhaps they are struck by the power of the spires, the glory of the windows; but they have known God, after all, longer than I have known him, and in a different way, and I am terrified by the slippery bottomless well to be found in the crypt, down which heretics were hurled to death, and by the obscene, inescapable gargoyles jutting out of the stone and seeming to say that God and the devil can never be divorced. I doubt that the villagers think of the devil when they face a cathedral because they have never been identified with the devil. But I must accept the status which myth, if nothing else, gives me in the West before I can hope to change the myth.

And this as a speculation on identity, even temporary identity, is full of imaginative promise. It suggests a coherence of psychological and social insight — exactly, that of an underground man. But then it is only half an imaginative statement, a parenthesis in an essay which demands a development of a different kind of truth. Baldwin doesn't indulge or sustain it. It is only a face for a moment put on identity to make it frightening, much like the image that, Baldwin says elsewhere, Richard Wright created in Bigger Thomas. Bigger asserts his "identity" by making manifest the brutal American image of the Negro. But Bigger isn't, Baldwin goes on in that essay to say, the Negro's identity—and neither, it is by the same token to be seen, is the devil—but only one of his roles, and it is a role which, Baldwin says, being all responsive hatred, marks the surrender of the Negro's identity.

The fact that he is forced to contain roles, at an extremity that role proposed by Bigger or the devil and ordinarily a role in a routine of daily cunning in his relations with whites, suggests at times what would seem for Baldwin to be at least a condition of the Negro's identity. The Negro ordinarily, Baldwin says again and again, is forced to consider whites much more intensely than they consider him, and he is forced to strategies in his dealings with them. "This is, indeed, one of the causes of the bottomless anger of black men: that they have been forced to learn far more about whites than whites have ever found it necessary to learn about them." And he says, "since white men represent in the black men's world so heavy a weight, white men have for black men a reality which is far from being reciprocal. . . . " The consequences of that fact, as Baldwin develops them sporadically in various places, are that the Negro invests much of his life in outwitting white people, and that the Negro bears toward white people an attitude which is designed to rob them of their naïveté. And it is an associated fact that Negroes are almost always acting.

This very virtuosity, one would think, might establish for Baldwin the grounds of the identity he seeks. The image of his hero might be located anywhere on an arc from the Confidence Man, or, for that matter, Rinehart, to Tyll Eulenspiegel. In fact the hero as trickster does occupy an occasional place in his fiction, which is always about identity. The hero of "Previous Condition of Servitude," Baldwin's earliest published story, tells a white friend, first, that it was part of his earliest education to learn how to act with policemen—"I let my jaw drop and I let my eyes get big. I didn't give him any smart answers, none of the crap about my rights"—and then:

> There are times and places when a Negro can use his color like a shield. He can trade on the subterranean Anglo-Saxon guilt and get what he wants that way; or some of what he wants. He can trade on his nuisance value, his value as forbidden fruit; he can use it like a knife, he can twist it and get his vengeance that way.

And in a story twelve years later, called "This Morning, This Evening, So Soon," the Negro hero sits again with a white friend and tells him again that a Negro must know how to act with policemen and he makes again, in effect, the consequent generalization. He is, of course, the same hero.

It is significant that despite twelve years and changed circumstances he is the same hero, that the same episode and the same observations are repeated and not developed. This trickery by which Baldwin says his hero lives is a shocking thing, but not so shocking apparently that it really becomes part of him. It doesn't change his life. He is still free to see it. It doesn't contribute to his identity, but in fact it is another of the special circumstances that prevents identity. His heroes don't *want* to be tricksters, and despite the fact that they say they practice tricks, they don't act like tricksters. They want to manifest *themselves*. The young man of "Previous Condition of Servitude" continues:

> I knew these things long before I realized that I knew them and
> in the beginning I used them, not knowing what I was doing. Then
> when I began to see it, I felt betrayed. I felt beaten as a person.
> I had no honest place to stand.

This middling-young man of "This Morning, This Evening, So Soon" comes to the end of his observations on trickery by saying, "I always feel that I don't exist there [in America], except in someone else's—usually dirty—mind." Trickery doesn't create a trickster. It robs the hero of himself. It is not even an activity, but a plight, a falsification which frustrates the something within.

The something within is something prior to all the pressures of large social determination and to a man's action in the large world. This humanity which cannot be categorized might then take its shape from more intimate pressures, those of the family and of ancestry, from the pressures of the Negro neighborhood and of the folk tradition. The Negro family, it turns out in Baldwin's fiction, is another conspiracy to prevent identity, but meanwhile those fictions—as distinct from the personal essays—in which Baldwin most obviously commits himself personally, do take the family and the Negro environment for their setting. The folk tradition is in his fiction, too, and it promises another condition of identity.

The expression of identity might be in the music of Negro folk tradition. An essay, which is for the most part about *Native Son*, begins: "It is only in his music, which Americans are able to admire because a protective sentimentality limits their understanding of it, that the Negro in America has been able to tell his story," and as an aid to the telling of his version of it, Baldwin has used Negro musical motifs here and there throughout his work. His titles are almost as often as not fragments of spirituals and blues: "Many Thousands Gone," "Nobody Knows My Name," "This Morning, This Evening, So Soon," "Come Out the Wilderness," *The Fire Next Time*. *Go Tell It on the Mountain* uses the spiritual of the title and uses fragments from a number of other spirituals as a binding device. There is at least by such reference a presence of Negro music in Baldwin's work. The music contributes a tone, and that tone at the very least reinforces the yearning that anyway is in much of the work. The music projects a style, which may contain an identity. Negro music has specific character, and by appealing to it Baldwin does manage to borrow something, at the very least a useful ornamentation.

But then if there is within the tone and the style and the character of Negro music a deep secret of identity, something literal and certain but something which Americans are unable really to understand, Baldwin does not reveal it. His one most thorough use of the music of Negro tradition is in his story called "Sonny's Blues." The story is largely an attempt to translate the blues into the terms of fiction. It fails to do that, perhaps for the sufficient reason that music doesn't translate, but it does seem to arrive at a statement of the Negro motives that may issue in the blues. Sonny's brother, a respectable Negro and a schoolteacher, tells the story. He has fallen out of touch with Sonny, who is not respectable, and through the story he is to come to understand and to regain his brother. Sonny is a young Negro caught on the one hand between the degradations, the slumminess of Harlem, and on the other hand the bourgeois, white ambitions of the relatives among whom he finds himself. Sonny's problem is precisely the burden of his racial identity: he must keep himself from drowning in the degradations and sorrows of Negro life, but something within him demands also that he be "with it," meaning, within the bounds of the story, that he not be white, that he acknowledge his racial community. The Negro community has offered him first heroin, a temporary escape from the feeling of degradation and slumminess. But he has discovered that the same environment contains a music, jazz, and through jazz he is to be provided with the means of reconciliation. The function of Sonny's blues is that it allows him fully to know his racial identity. At the end of the story his brother listens to Sonny's piano, and thinks:

> He had made it his: that long line, of which we knew only Mama and Daddy. And he was giving it back, as everything must be given back, so that, passing through death, it can live forever. I saw my mother's face again, and felt, for the first time, how the stones of the road she had walked on must have bruised her feet. I saw the moonlit road where my father's brother died. . . . And I was yet aware that this was only a moment, that the world waited outside, as hungry as a tiger, and that trouble stretched above us, longer than the day.

The story of the Negro that the music tells is of ancient sorrows somehow borne, that may be borne still in a world that still confers suffering. That is what Negro-ness is. Or that is what it might be. But then the significance of this lyrical statement really is in the fact that nothing in the story serves to make it true. The music is another of Baldwin's promises of identity that is not paid. It is significant that it is Sonny's brother, the schoolteacher, the would-be white man, and not Sonny, who tells this story and who translates the message of the blues. Sonny's brother is the man most in need of reconciliation and most in need of the blues. And it happens that what he observes about the music is quite superfluous to anything he has in the story learned about it, just as what he hears in Sonny's playing is less important dramatically than the fact that he hears it and responds. Sonny is from the beginning full of unspecified Negro-ness, and that is the difference between the brothers. The protagonist comes, we are to believe, to some implicit understanding of Sonny's suffering, and then, at the climax, when he hears the music, the magic is worked. The dramatic impact of the story, that is to say, is not in his understanding of anything that is in the music, but in his reconciliation with what his brother in the first place vaguely represents. What he says he understands in the music is unimportant. Any message of reconciliation would have worked as well. And all that the climax really proves by showing it on stage is the wordless communicativeness that is in the music, and the direct and spontaneous communicativeness that is especially the strategy of jazz.

It is directness and spontaneity of expression that in this story of identity is finally referred to, and not any content of tradition. And it is something very much like that that Baldwin discovers when he pursues the folk tradition in other directions, into the South or to Africa. He has made this pursuit infrequently but he has made it sometimes, and with some promising. The essay "Nobody Knows My Name" begins: "Negroes in the North are right when they refer to the South as the Old Country." The Northern Negro "sees, in effect, his ancestors, who, in everything they do and are, proclaim his inescapable identity." The American Negro, Baldwin says elsewhere, has been significantly separated from his African antecedents, but nevertheless they are part of him. "I know . . . that the most crucial time in my own development came when I was forced to recognize that I was a kind of bastard of the West; when I followed the line of my past I did not find myself in Europe but in Africa." "Go back a few centuries," he says again, "and . . . I am in Africa, watching the conquerors arrive." Here, then, in the South or, behind it, in Africa, is a hint of identity. And especially if it is true that experience obscures identity, in this primitive incarnation identity should be apparent.

It is not, as Baldwin presents it, immediately apparent, but it is, precisely, primitive. "The American image of the Negro lives also in the Negro's heart," Baldwin says once, and here, in his discovery of Negroes, as it were, darker than he, he presents some proof of it. The Negro of the Old Country is as he appears in Baldwin's essays, for the most part a militant engaged in the current heightened battle of the South, and so questions of his distinguishing identity are not distinctly raised. But there are hints. On the occasion of what he records as his first visit to the South, in "Nobody Knows My Name," Baldwin observes of the "familiar" landscape: "What passions cannot be unleashed on a dark road in a Southern night! Everything seems so sensual, so languid, and so private." The school integration dispute has nothing to do with education, but it "has to do with political power and it has to do with sex." And in fact the underlying metaphor of the whole of this fictive essay is sexual. Only its overt observations have to do with political power. The distinguishing thing about these Old Country Negroes is that they are living a history that is covertly sexual.

And in one of the few stories that deals at all with the South, "Come Out the Wilderness," there is the same tugging suggestion, that sex *is* the Old Country identity. The heroine, in this case, has just come out of the South to what she thinks of as the gray rigidities and the meaningless abstractions and the cruelty and confusion of Manhattan. She has come, so an explicitly Freudian content of the story suggests, bearing the burden of an explicitly sexual trauma. She is living now with a white man. She is thereby obsessively punishing herself. Her brother once had caught her in a compromising situation and said to her, "You dirty . . . you black and dirty." Black is therefore the color of sex, and in her affair she is exploiting her blackness and her carnality. And both, the story keeps suggesting, are products of her Southernness. She has relatives in Harlem who have, by moving to Harlem, become respectably and repressively religious. The Northern Negro women among whom she works have a cold sterility about them. She is herself a person of high moral awareness, but as she is Southern she is more black and so her morality is different; she is pure, and it is the mark of her purity that she is sexual.

The South also prevents or corrupts expression, sexual or otherwise. That is a part of the story of *Go Tell It on the Mountain*, and of some of the essays. But the ur-, pre-Northern Negro as the incarnation of uncorrupted identity does occupy some part of Baldwin's imagination. The Southern Negro and, more notably, the African, have preserved a cultural and therefore a psychic wholeness. "The African . . . has endured privation, injustice, medieval cruelty; but the African has not yet endured the utter alienation of himself from his people and his past. His mother did not sing 'Sometimes I Feel Like a Motherless Child.' . . . " And then the mark of this wholeness, again in the case of the African, is undifferentiated sexual energy. Baldwin says it between the lines, but he says it. In an essay, "Encounter on the Seine," about the attitude of American

Negroes, which is to say of Baldwin, toward the North African students at the Sorbonne, the drama of the encounter fills momentarily with jungle rhythms. The American Negro faces the African before him, and: "Yet, as he wishes for a moment that he were home again, where at least the terrain is familiar, there begins to race within him, like the despised beat of the tom-tom, echoes of a past which he has not yet been able to utilize, intimations of a responsibility which he has not yet been able to face." Then, in a parenthesis in an epitaph for Richard Wright, Baldwin remarks that when an American Negro "faces an African, he is facing the unspeakably dark, guilty, erotic past which the Protestant fathers made him bury . . . but which lives in his personality and haunts the universe yet." And the conception of the African as dark, as the darker brother, as mysteriously guilty, as secretly erotic, lurks, if it does not always come to expression, somewhere in whatever Baldwin says about Africans.

It is with the Southern Negro and the African, who don't after all occupy him very much, that Baldwin makes his longest reach toward an identifiable identity. Writing as he does so exclusively out of himself, they of course wouldn't, except in a speculative way, occupy him very much, but that they do at all take a place in his drama of the search for identity provides the clearest indication of the nature of the goal. It is not roots that Baldwin seeks, as it is not the product of any particular response to any particular life. It is merely something that has been buried. It is something that will reveal itself when the individual is stripped of particularity. It will therefore be felt, if still not seen, only in moments of ungoverned passion, in pure hating and pure loving— and it is therefore, in Baldwin's fiction, bound to fail of achievement. Fiction has the techniques to accomplish the departure from Eden and the coming of worldliness. Innocence travels toward experience. And worldliness is a drama of perpetual qualifying, just such a one as Baldwin sometimes does complain of. So, he says, the Negro in his relations with white Americans is prohibited "anything so uncomplicated and satisfactory as pure hatred." On the other hand, the characters of Baldwin's fiction are prohibited anything so uncomplicated as pure loving. Or when they are not prohibited, as is the case particularly in some moments of *Another Country*, the fiction surrenders to rhapsody.

It is the search for purity that is the scheme of Baldwin's fiction. The "identity" of his heroes is finally without form. It was Bellow's Augie March who started with the faith that a man's character is his fate, but he ended with the lesson that a man's fate is his character. Augie's moral engagement with the world identifies him. Baldwin's drama is premoral. The problem of his heroes is rather the pure transmission of pure impulse. They can neither hate nor love because their world—the world itself—is complicated and imposes limitations. They are therefore lonely in the world, and therefore pitiable. The world closes in on them, and their responsive action is either surrender to themselves, a turning inward, or, in the attempt to burst out of their isolation, they take to bizarre and extreme expression of the impulse within.

The deep problems of accommodation are always just around the corner and waiting for Baldwin's heroes. They constitute the reason for Baldwin's writing. They are not met because Baldwin's heroes end their adventures in a cry of loneliness, or in incredible pathos. But then, despite the fact that Baldwin has heroes of various colors practicing their heroism variously, in narratives that look like essays and in narratives that are fiction, it is not anyone's loneliness which engages Baldwin. He is concerned with his own, and his deepest and most promising work has been in that fiction that has drawn specifically on an identity which, willy-nilly, he does have.

PHILIP ROTH

Blues for Mr. Charlie

In the brief note James Baldwin has written as an introduction to the published version of *Blues for Mr. Charlie*, the only character he mentions at any length is the man appearing in the play as Lyle Britten, a white storeowner in a Southern town who murders a young Negro. Baldwin says of the killer, "We have the duty to try to understand this wretched man." But in the play that follows, the writer's sense of this particular duty seems to me to fail him. The compassionate regard for the character that Baldwin means to convey by the adjective "wretched" is not the same quality of emotion that informs his imagination when he is examining the man in his wretchedness. Being dutiful to the murderer is not Baldwin's overriding moral impulse. Rather, a conflict of impulses—duties towards a variety of causes, of which, unfortunately, the cause of art seems to have inspired the weakest loyalty—prevents Baldwin from fixing his attention upon his subject and increasing "understanding," his or ours. I think of this Introduction (dated April 1964) as an attempt by the writer to remember where it was he may have begun, for that is not where he has ended. I don't intend to hold a play deficient for failing an intention whose execution may properly have been thwarted in the act of writing, and is perhaps only recalled here in nostalgia for some purity of purpose. The deficiency is in the failure to be true not to the particular intention announced in the Introduction, but to those numerous intentions apparent in the first act, all most worthy, but none able to survive the unhealthy competition.

The play begins with the murder of the Negro Richard Henry, a young man who has returned to the South from New York, where he started out

From *The New York Review of Books* 2, no. 8 (May 28, 1964). © 1964 by The New York Review, Inc. Originally entitled "Channel X: Two Plays on the Race Conflict."

as a jazz musician and ended up as a junkie. The man who shoots him, Lyle
Britten, owns a country store which returns him little profit in good times,
and is now returning hardly any because of a Negro boycott. Britten is a simple,
ignorant young man married to a simple and ignorant young woman; they
have a baby they love and friends who are fond of them and who, like the
Brittens, are baffled and angered by the demonstrations, the marches, the
boycotts, organized by the Negroes in the town. Britten and Richard meet
shortly after Richard's arrival back home. Instantly Lyle hates Richard for being
black and arrogant, as Richard hates him for being white and arrogant—and
for being a killer too, for Lyle had already murdered a colored man years ago
and gone unpunished for it. After a couple of accidental but angry encounters,
culminating in Richard knocking Lyle down in front of his wife, the white
man comes hunting the black man with a gun.

It is the shots fired from this gun that open the play. When the curtain
rises, we see Lyle carrying the dead Negro over his shoulder; he dumps him
to the ground and says, "And may every nigger like this nigger end like this
nigger—face down in the weeds!" He exits, and now the play begins again:
the time is the day before the funeral of Richard Henry, the place is a Negro
church in the town, whose minister is Reverend Meridian Henry, the father
of the dead young man. The action moves forward from this moment through
Richard's funeral in act 2, to the scandalous trial and eventual acquittal of Lyle
Britten which comprises almost all of act 3. But it also moves backward in
a series of flashbacks which begins with Richard's arrival in town and goes
on to reveal the events leading up to his murder. If by the end of the play
this flashing backwards has become nothing more than a mechanical device
used to fill us in on historical data that is either unimportant or uninteresting,
in the first act it seems a genuine inspiration of form. For the direction the
play takes is an expression of the will of one of the characters, Richard's father,
who searches for the meaning of this murder for himself, for his son, and for
the man who committed it. Unlike his son, Reverend Meridian Henry believes
that the dignity of his race is not served by violence; he despises injustice no
less than Richard, but his passion to gain his people their rights is subsumed
by the passion to save souls, not for the next world either, but for this one.

Consequently Richard returns home to a father whose values can only
anger him. As the scenes move back in time, we learn that Richard, who died
by another's violence, had come home prepared to protect himself against such
violence. He had returned armed with a gun, and now, in the past, we hear
him say that he will use it in his own defense if he has to. He has supposedly
been demoralized by his failure in the North (ending in the narcotics cure at
Lexington) and this demoralization only feeds his ancient hatred of the white

man. It was the white men lusting after his mother who one day pushed her down a flight of stairs to her death; Richard's departure from home was in part an attempt to leave that horrid memory behind, and to leave his father, whose powerlessness before such humiliations he had come to hate as well. He is rich with anger, and yet in the very first scene with his father, he surrenders to him the pistol he has brought back with him from the North, an act for which he will in the end have to pay with his life.

Why does he surrender the pistol? Meridian himself does not demand it, although his values may seem to. Instead, at his son's provocation, Meridian admits that the mother was in fact pushed, and did not slip as apparently he had once tried to make his son believe. Richard now gives him the gun supposedly because Meridian has given up the truth, and given it up to him. But this truth his father speaks only verifies what Richard had already known. Surrendering the gun at this point, then, is either psychological perversity on Richard's part (a clue to a motive of which he himself is unaware), or sentimentality on the part of the writer, who may so want a scene of loving and forgiveness between a father and a son on the stage that he will have one even if it means destroying the most authentic facts about his own characters. Or else it is just so much piety about that word *truth*. Whatever the cause, at the most important dramatic moment of the act (and maybe of the play) the sense of the drama is hopelessly distorted: Meridian Henry, rather than disputing his son's judgment of him, accepts it, asks to be forgiven; and Richard, instead of finding his strength of purpose hardened by his father's truthfulness, surrenders his purpose by surrendering the gun. At whom then was his fury directed in the first place? Against whom was the gun to protect him? The white men who murdered his mother (and might try murdering him) or the father whose illusions he believes allowed her to be murdered?

These complexities of motive are hardly uninteresting, but in this instance have less to do with the play than with the playwright. They may even tell us that beneath the play presented, there is a hidden play about a Negro father and a Negro son—a drama that did not really come to light, but may perhaps have spread a kind of haze over the writer's imagination which only further confused his purpose. How telling, how unclouded, the scene between father and son, if Meridian were with Richard the man he is with the Negro students in the brief but brilliantly ironic opening scene where he is seen firing at them abusive epithets and insults, pretending to be the worst of white men in order to turn them into what he truly believes are the best of the black: men of iron self-control who will not weaken to violence. How to the point of what the play at first appears to be about, if Meridian had said, "You cannot live in my house with a gun"; if Richard had replied, "That's how you killed my

mother"—and if Meridian had answered, "You are wrong. I want the gun."
Then that struggle which also seems to remain confused in the heart of the
writer, the struggle between love and hate, would have been untangled in the
drama, even if it could not, and cannot, be resolved for either the playwright
or the audience. But this required the dramatist to permit one of his characters
to become a hero, and his play, perhaps, to aspire to tragedy. For a while,
I thought Baldwin had chosen Meridian to fill the role of tragic hero in what
is really a tragic story. If he had, then real blues might have been sung in the
end for the Negro rather than those spurious blues for Mr. Charlie, who is
the white man, and who can hardly be said to be the play's hero either.

The first act does present a white man Baldwin may originally have thought
of as his suffering hero, however; or one he might have allowed to be. He
is Parnell James, the editor of the local newspaper, a buddy to Lyle Britten,
the murderer, and a friend to Meridian Henry as well as the other Negroes
of the town. It is Parnell James who arranges that Lyle be brought to trial,
a betrayal which Lyle does not resent since apparently (and incredibly) his feelings
of betrayal are negated by his understanding that no jury of white men is going
to convict him. But Parnell betrays his buddy for his friend—and his principles.
Having taken his first righteous action, he is pushed by Meridian to go further.
Meridian demands that Parnell make Lyle admit to him what he will not admit
to the court, that he killed Richard. When Parnell replies, "Meridian—what
you ask—I don't know if I can do it for you," the minister answers, "I don't
want you to do it for me. I want you to do it for you." Here the first act ends.

Why the drama of the past has been running parallel to the drama of the
present is suddenly made clear. Both courses of action begin in the force exerted
by the preacher on two different men: the first his son Richard—by accepting
his gun the preacher sets in motion the drama that is to end in Richard's dying
unprotected; the second his friend. For if anybody is to be saved by Richard's
death perhaps it is this white man who may have it in his power to cause
the murderer and the town "to face the evil that it countenances and to turn
from evil and do good." To Meridian, Parnell is the one who may yet save
them all. So the act ends, with the minister putting to the test one last time
his faith in the possibility of salvation through moral instruction—through words.
One would think that the rest of the play will be devoted to Parnell's struggle,
as the action proceeds in the present, and to Richard's struggle—living without
a gun—in the past.

But in the remaining two acts of the play all the purposes of the first act
collapse; indeed, everything collapses, sense, craft, and feeling. The duty to
understand is replaced with a duty to do what is practically its opposite, to
propagandize, or (reversing Blake's dictum) "to put off intellect and put on

holiness." Hardly anything anyone has said or done to anyone else in act 1 seems to have taken hold, and the not taking hold isn't what is made to seem the point, either. The point is that the writer has pronouncements to make which stand in the way of the play he began to write. The issue of the gun, for instance, disappears, and as for the conversation with the father, it might as well never have happened. Richard's struggle against hatred never materializes (he falls in love instead), nor does Parnell's against the moral blindness of Lyle Britten (he just sits around listening to Britten). Consequently the will of Meridian Henry is quickly snuffed out, and he too disappears as an important force in the drama. When the curtain goes up on act 2 the circumstances and the people of act 1 are pretty much swept aside. Now we are over in Whitetown, in the home of Lyle Britten, who is the murderer, but not the villain—as, in a way, Richard is the victim without being the hero. Both are dummies who only move their mouths while the real hero and villain air their views. For the real hero of these last two acts is blackness, as the real villain is whiteness.

If there is ever a Black Muslim nation, and if there is television in that nation, then something like acts 2 and 3 of *Blues for Mr. Charlie* will probably be the kind of thing the housewives will watch on afternoon TV. It is soap opera designed to illustrate the superiority of blacks over whites. The blues Baldwin may think he is singing for Mr. Charlie's sinning seem to me really to be sung for his inferiority. First, Negroes are better looking, particularly Negro women. When the white men in the play claim *They're after our women!* they are obviously having guilt-ridden fantasies: almost every Negro man around would testify, and almost everyone does, that white women are cold, unappealing, "pasty-faced bitches"—particularly Richard, who for all his promiscuity with the pasty-faces of New York, is well-cured of such frivolous lust by the time he appears back home; that is, on the stage. On the other hand, when the Negro students (mostly the Negroes are students; mostly the whites are plain old crackers) reply *You're after ours!* the play then "proves" this to be true. The only sexual affairs of real consequence to Lyle Britten and Parnell James were with Negro women—Lyle with a girl both pretty and passionate, and Parnell with a girl in possession of both these qualities, plus a third: she was a reader. The first time he came upon her alone she was poring over *The Red and the Black* in the library. Negroes then, even studious ones, make love better. They dance better. And they cook better. And their penises are longer, or stiffer. Indeed, so much that comprises the Southern stereotype of the Negro comes back through Negro mouths as testimony to their human superiority, that finally one is about ready to hear that the eating of watermelon increases one's word power. It is as though the injustice of our racial situation is that inferiors are enslaving their superiors, rather than the other way around.

The man who most indulges in this self-congratulation is Richard Henry, and in Baldwin's defense, it can be said that Richard's opinions don't represent the range of Baldwin's own ideas and feelings. But surely these ideas and feelings are what determine the perspective in which Baldwin presents Richard to us. In fact, what I find most disturbing in the play are not these patently defensive opinions of Richard's, but the value that Baldwin imagines accrues to Richard's own humanity by the deeds that grow out of his opinions. Much as I object to Baldwin's psychologizing about why Richard is what he is, I object even more to his moralizing about Richard's worth. At the very moment Baldwin seems to feel that Richard has risen above his opinions to a kind of vengeful manliness, it seems to me that he has sunk beneath them and is their victim. This moment occurs in the second act, in the scene which establishes the dramatic cause for the murder. Richard enters Lyle Britten's store for a Coke and sets out to provoke his wife by offering to pay for the drink with a twenty-dollar bill; he continues to provoke and insult her even though Lyle comes in from the back of the store carrying a hammer. Lyle is supposed to be carrying the hammer because he is making some repairs somewhere, but I believe he is really carrying it so that he can raise it to Richard when he refuses to leave the store, and so that Richard can then throw him to the ground despite the disadvantage of being without a weapon. So that Richard, in short, can emerge as heroic in his anger, to both his friend Lorenzo, who is waiting outside, and to the audience. But why isn't it his girl friend Juanita who is waiting outside, or his father? After all, in act 1 Juanita says, with passion, "I won't let you go anywhere without me." I would think that if either of these characters had been present, if act 1 had taken hold of the writer himself, then Richard could not have appeared to be heroic, but might have had to be seen for what he is — pathetic in his adolescent masculine pride, no less than Lyle Britten in his. Watching this scene one is as uncomfortable for the playwright as one might be listening to the boastings of a schoolboy who dishes up to you as the hard facts of his adventurous and daring life what are actually daydreams of sexual heroism.

His making a hero of blackness, combined with his sentimentalizing of masculinity, blinds Baldwin to the fact that Richard's condition is no less hideously comic than Lyle Britten's. There is no glory or hope, not a shred of it, to be found in the life of either the black man or the white. What these characters give evidence to, what the play seems to be about really, is the small-mindedness of the male sex. It is about the narcissistic, pompous, and finally ridiculous demands made by the male ego when confronted by moral catastrophe. Of course to take pride in one's maleness, as so many of the men in this play would like to do, is hardly ridiculous; but to identify this maleness with the size and capabilities of one's penis is to reveal about as much depth of imagination as I remember finding one long Saturday afternoon among my colleagues in an Army motor pool. It is shattering (and not as the writer intends so obviously for it to be) to hear the young Negro woman, Juanita, announce to the audience at the close of act 2 in the most stirring tones, "And I'll see the world again—the marvelous world. And I'll have learned from Richard— how to love." From *Richard?* Richard's boasting about being black and brag- ging about his penis have blinded somebody to the truth about him, which is that neither he, nor Lyle, for that matter, is a wretched man; they only behave wretchedly. They are banal men who suffer most their own banality. In fact, *A Study in the Banality of Evil* would have been a title more to the. point of the play that Baldwin has actually written than *Blues for Mr. Charlie.*

CHARLES NEWMAN

The Lesson of the Master:
Henry James and James Baldwin

The moral is that the flower of art blooms only where the soil is deep, that it takes a great deal of history to produce a little literature, that it needs a complex social machinery to set a writer in motion.

— HENRY JAMES

James Baldwin has made a reputation by exploiting social paradoxes, so it should not be surprising to trace his literary antecedents to neither Richard Wright nor Harriet B. Stowe, but to that Brahmin, Henry James. Consider this sentence, for example:

> For what, at bottom, distinguished the Americans from the Negroes who surrounded us, men from Nigeria, Barbados, Martinique—so many names for so many disciplines—was the banal and quite overwhelming fact that we had been born in a society which, in a way quite inconceivable for Africans, and no longer real for Europeans, was open, and in a sense, which has nothing to do with justice or injustice, was free.

The amphibian elegance of such syntax comes naturally to an artist obsessed by dualities, paradox. The Atlantic Ocean separated James's mind into opposed hemispheres, and the gulf of color so cleaves Baldwin. The antipodes of their worlds propose a dialectical art.

Such patent oppositions often prove disastrous in fiction, insofar as they

From *The Yale Review* 56, no. 1 (October 1966). © 1966 by Yale University.

tend to oversimplify character and conflict. So, to be fair, it should be noted at the outset that Baldwin's characters suffer no more from their color than James's suffer from their money—these are only the peculiar conditions of their suffering. The problem for both is more universal—the opacity of their culture and the question of their identity within it. For Baldwin assumes, in the consequences of his culture, the crisis of his identity, the reflective burden of Western Man. His color is his metaphor, his vantage. But in his despair, he is closer to Henry Adams than John Henry.

Both Baldwin and James were victims of a "mysterious childhood accident." Only their society's different reaction to puberty sets them apart. It is not so much a question of how it happened, but the consequences. "I'm the reaction against the mistake," says Lambert Strether in *The Ambassadors*, and Baldwin certifies this most finally for his contemporaries. "They were so other," James elaborates in *A Small Boy and Others*, "that was what I felt; and to be other, *other almost anyhow*, seemed as good as the probable taste of the bright compound wistfully watched in the confectioner's window" (emphasis mine).

Their hurts are obscure only because such wounds are generally ignored by those enamored of the big candy in the window. The pose necessitated is that of the *powerless, feeling young man*. The psychological consequence is self-imposed exile; to be "other almost anyhow." The literary consequence is the novel of "manners" (read prejudice); this being the drama of how personal histories conflict with the public history of the time. Personal action can only be understood in terms of its public consequences. Morality, in this sense, may not be relative, but it is always comparative.

The two exiles share a further insight. Both writers realized early that the American fabric is not subject to European tailoring, that America has no culture in European terms. But as James said, "The American knows that a good deal remains; what is it that remains—that is his secret, his joke, as one may say. . . . "

The "secret" is evident in the invalidism of their public poses, their exile *in order* to communicate. One learns about America, not from being in Europe as much as from *not* being in America. But this exile, this rebellious detachment, has ambiguous consequences. On the one hand, it affects a dialectical viewpoint, which is to say, it sees the world in terms of primary conflicts. On the other hand, the very symmetry, the *given* drama of such polar conflicts, may be so compelling as to preclude any further analysis or development. A comparison of these two exiles, their experience with the dialectic, not only reflects the cultural history of a half-century, but implies a good deal about the future of the novel.

Baldwin's first paradox is that he uses the Negro, uses him ruthlessly, to show the White Man what the White Man is. Repeatedly in his work, he returns to that image of a Negro hung from a fine Southern tree with his sex cut out. We confront the Negro, we cannot miss him. But we know little about him except that he suffered. We know more, implicitly, about the White Man who left him there. The insights and blind spots of such a technique are illustrated in Baldwin's most ambitious work, *Another Country*.

This novel is populated by a series of characters, or rather couples, as geometrically entangled as Far Eastern erotic sculpture, the only undocumented relationship being that unlovely norm—monogamous, heterosexual marriage. Consider the cast of characters:

Rufus: black jazz drummer, attempts to surmount his ghetto existence by a love affair with a Southern poor white, *Leona*. The attempt to confront, transcend, their past results in her madness and his suicide. This couple is removed from the action relatively early. Subsequent relationships embellish this dazzling affair from other sexual and moral perspectives, through the use of *ficelles*—James's word for characters who, while not self-sustaining, provide *relief* or depth by their juxtaposition to the primary figures of the work.

Vivaldo: white Irish-Italian, unpublished writer, has an affair with *Rufus*'s sister, panther-lady, jazz singer, *Ida*. Tempered, perhaps, by the knowledge that their respective talents may gain them escape from the ghetto, *Ida* and *Vivaldo* seem one generation removed from the heat of *Rufus* and *Leona*. They are reincarnations; history is personalized for them through the primary disastrous affair. To some extent, Vivaldo overcomes Leona's naïveté; Ida, her brother's cynicism. "You got to pay your dues," is Ida's theme—and although nothing is resolved, we suspect that in willing to be haunted, they may yet finally afford it.

Then there is *Cass*, blonde upper-class Anglo-Saxon; and her husband, *Richard*, blonde lower-class Polack, high school teacher of Vivaldo, writer. What Cass comes to resent in her husband is not clear—he is disciplined rather than talented perhaps—he does not indulge in the other's frenetic search for a large identity—he actually finishes a book and gets it published. In any case, *Cass* has an affair with *Eric*, ex-Alabama actor, formerly a lover of Rufus and later involved with Vivaldo, then in an interlude awaiting the arrival of his present lover, *Yves*, French, ex-male prostitute. This affair is necessarily brief. *Cass* gets guilty and tells *Richard*; the question of revenge is made properly irrelevant by the knowledge that he has been cuckolded by a queer. We leave him searching out *Vivaldo*, ready to take up, apparently, the aimless rebellion the rest of them find so compelling, the source of his stability defiled. Meanwhile, *Cass* and *Eric* arrange their *Te Deum* in the Museum of Modern Art. The scene is crucial and among the best in the book.

"Dear Cass . . . how are you?
"Dead . . ."
"You picked a strange place for us to meet . . ."
"Did I? I just couldn't think of any other place."

And with this they move through the unending anterooms of the modern
world—all glass and steel, no texture there—rooms emblazoned with incom-
prehensible abstractions, cold walls ogled by triumphant myopics, ". . . like
tourists in a foreign graveyard." Before an enormous red canvas, stand a boy
and girl holding hands, American Gothic against the Apocalypse.

Here, in one scene, is all that distance between Christopher Newman,
James's *American*, and more contemporary stuff. For despite Newman's inability to accept his own culture or to fathom a foreign atmosphere no less
stifling, he could find solace in the red doors of Notre Dame, as James did
in the *Galerie d'Appallon*. By simply standing in the Bellegarde's great hall,
Newman could construe the nature of his rebuff; that it was his part to pay
his absentee rent and return home.

That is the nostalgic quality of James's characters—they divine their
atmosphere, their responses are equal to the situation. They make their peace
with a precise if unhappy destiny. But the atmosphere is more opaque for
Baldwin's characters, it elicits no response, they simply suffer from it. The
museum is no longer teaching machine or urban oasis, any more than bank
or hospital, church or train station—their sensitivity, their culture, their very
cosmopolitanism is turned against them.

Through this Cass moves, "small, pale, and old-fashioned in her hood . . .
disenchanted." Eric "wished that he could rescue her, that it was in his power
to make her life less hard. But it was only love which could accomplish the
miracle of making a life bearable—only love, and love itself hopelessly failed;
and he had never loved her. He had used her to find something out about
himself. *And even this was not true.* He had used her in the hope of avoiding
a confrontation with himself."

Cass is pithy as any Jamesian interlocutor. "He can suffer, after all," she
says of Richard. "I told him because . . . that if we were going to—continue
together—we could begin on a new basis with everything clear between us.
But I was wrong—some things cannot be clear . . . or perhaps some things *are*
clear, only one won't face those things."

In that parallelism hangs the book. Tolstoy would have used those last
sentences as his first. The story would have unfolded from their dichotomy.
It is characteristic of modern art that the thesis is not hung until we have been
dragged kicking through every conceivable blind alley—the self being the sum
of the destruction of all false selves.

Echoes of these three relationships reverberate through another series of *ficelles*. Eric and Yves *en famille* in France, Eric and Vivaldo together for a night, Vivaldo's affair with *Jane*, a no-account painter, and Ida's with *Ellis*, a white promoter. Ellis and Jane are coupled as the whores, respectively, of the Commercial and Bohemian worlds. "To have one's pleasure without paying for it," Baldwin says elsewhere, "is precisely the way to find oneself reduced to a search for pleasure which grows steadily more desperate and more grotesque." Baldwin once accused Richard Wright of substituting violence for sex. He has come full circle.

In the end, things are magnificently unresolved, save for Rufus's death and Leona's madness. Vivaldo and Ida keep at their work, their respective therapies, having very little time left to make it before the defensiveness of Greenwich Village will crush them, too. Cass and Richard have "awoken," only to find themselves "dead." Undoubtedly, their children will keep them together formally, and Richard will halfheartedly take up the rebellion where Cass halfheartedly left it off. Jane finds security with an adman, and Ellis, excitement across the tracks in Harlem. Yves is coming and Eric's waiting. All end committed to nothing save the endurance of each other's better knowledge.

If this sounds flip, it is meant to be, for what makes modern tragedy most appalling is not its causality, but its very casualness. Here are the Jews boarding the box cars without resistance.

The irresolution of these destinies, however, has brought some critics down hard on Baldwin. The charge is formlessness. But if *Another Country* is formless, it has that in common with this nation's greatest literature. In the final scene, Eric goes to meet Yves at Idlewild.

> Yves... passed his examination with no trouble, and in a very short time; his passport was eventually stamped and handed back to him, with a grin and a small joke, the meaning but not the good nature of which escaped him. Then he was in a vaster hall, waiting for his luggage, with Eric above him, smiling down on him through glass. Then even his luggage belonged to him again, and he strode through the barriers, more highhearted than he had even been as a child, into that city which the people from heaven had made their home.

That is not the language of Henry James, the understated snippet of dialogue or restrained image which brings things to a close. It is the language of Gatsby and the Green Light, Huck Finn, "striking out for the territory," Ishmael, picked up, alone, to tell the tale—the picaresque open-end of American Literature. (As Robert A. Bone points out in a brilliant study, Baldwin, "in moments of high emotion," consistently reverts to his formal, more elaborate church-oriented narrative, rather than to any dialect or colloquial idiom.)

For a moment we are placated; he has gotten out of it in a traditional manner. But then we realize that in this ecstatic scene, no one is fleeing injustice with high hopes, Yves is no Lafayette on the beach; this is no rendezvous with destiny, but a discomforting liaison. The visionary rhetoric is utterly undercut.

So the legend of America as refuge for the oppressed, opportunity for the pure in heart, is invoked only to be exposed. From the very first, he is saying, our vision has been parochial. We have not accounted for the variety of man's motives, the underside of our settlers, the cost of a new life. The plague has come over as part of the baggage, and we will be sick until we isolate that cargo and deal with it. The back dues compound every day. If *Another Country* is formless, it is so because it rejects the theories of history available to it.

There is something further, however, an inadequacy which is worth pointing out, as it relates not only to Baldwin, but to modern literature itself.

What about the progenitors of such knowledge? The characters that set *Another Country* in motion, Leona and Rufus? It is what Baldwin does not know, or say, about them which is interesting, for they must bear the primary burden, they are the myth which the other couples mime. As myths, Baldwin tends to monumentalize them, give them stature by arresting their development. Like Greek royalty, their personality is gradually subsumed by the enormity of the crime which killed them.

But who are they? Rufus Scott has that ethereal sensitivity of the modern hero, half-adolescent, half-prophet, that *powerless, feeling young man* celebrated, apparently, because he rejects a success already denied him—the man who in Norman Mailer's words would "affect history by the sheer force of his sentiments." Or so the logic goes. But really, he is a monument from the very first, he is that Negro hanging from the tree with his sex cut out.

The fact is, that Rufus is nothing but his own potential, and the world is simply what thwarts it. He is a brilliantly rendered testament. But he is not a character. What *he* can't do and why *they* won't let him, is more vague than mysterious. He is, if you will, the Seymour Glass of his class, his virtue postulated by his lesser apostles. It is significant that although Rufus is a musician, we never hear him play. As with Seymour's alleged poetry, we await the aria that never comes.

And Leona? Poor white trash Isolde? Significantly, the only character in the book not devoted in some way to the arts. Symbols, representation, mean nothing to her. It is commerce, communication in the most direct sense, that she lives. "Do you love me?" everyman's saxophone asks. Leona says, "Don't hurt me." The pale white liberal; impotent (I ain't gonna have no more babies), platitudinous (it don't matter what two people's color is so long as they love each other), ineradicably guilty. She tries to love Rufus because she needs him, and he won't let her because it smacks of retribution. Her effort, pathetic, styleless, is for nothing. She is committed to an institution. But that is only the legal acknowledgment. If Baldwin does not see what Rufus might become, he does not see what Leona *is*. She does not go crazy; she has been mad from the beginning. As characters, they *go* nowhere; they die of nothing more than their own abstraction.

"What they (Negroes) hold in common is their precarious, their unutterably painful relation to the white world," Baldwin says. What the characters of *Another Country* hold in common is their precarious relation to a world which is defined by little more than its victims' resentment. One by one, we come upon them, hung from their respective trees, but the executioner never appears; like *Godot*, his name is simply invoked to "explain things." What is explicitly absent in Baldwin's politics—the differentiation between enemies, the priorities and strategies of rebellion—is implicitly absent in his literature.

To structure the dialogue in this way has its dramatic usefulness. The conflicts are elucidated in all their hopeless solipsism. But the consequence is also to make development, in terms of plot, psychology, or character, impossible. He is overwhelmed by the eloquence of his own dialectic. He has reached that moment which defines much of modern fiction—when the characters start to repeat themselves endlessly. Recapitulation of this sort has its irony—upon which the theatre of the absurd has capitalized—but artistically, it is also a dead end.

To understand how an artist can get into this situation, *Another Country* must be considered the result of a long and certainly uplifting process. Baldwin's progress as an artist has been his ability to articulate, confront, his central problems as a man and a writer. He tells us of his exile to Europe, with little but recordings of Bessie Smith and his shame. There, gradually, he came to grips with the central conflicts of his background, his love-hate affairs with religion, sex, color, America. In *Go Tell It on the Mountain*, the futile beauty of the Negro church is dealt with by incorporating its esthetic while rejecting it as an institution. He learns to use the jagged Negro folk poetry and religious rhetoric, to counter the urbane elegance of his Jamesian style. In *Giovanni's Room*, "the male prison" is dealt with as the "church-as-jail" by using the ambiguities of sexual desire as the proof-text for a larger rebellion. In *Notes of a Native Son*, in *Nobody Knows My Name*, Baldwin discovers himself further. What began as a crippling disgust with both his race and country, as an *American*, a *Negro*, becomes a subtle distinctive pride in each as *americanegro*. In these

essays, he finds a unique and telling voice—neither before nor since are his
categories so precisely focused, nor his language so controlled. He has "his secret,
his joke." He returns.

Such progress is apparent in *Another Country*, but it is a work of a different
order. It is less explicitly therapeutic, more ambitious. It is the very repetition,
the surface perversity of the encounters, that gradually makes perversity
irrelevant. For this is not at all a book about interracial affairs, homosexual
affairs, adulterous affairs, but about *affairs*—it evolves in the same way that
Portrait of a Lady, say, unfolds upon the loom of marriage. The various
approaches, styles, perspectives are secondary. They all need the same thing
if they face different obstacles, they all pay the same dues. Everyone hits bottom
in his own way and that is that. Yves and Eric's liaison is significant on one
level of irony, but ultimately it is of no peculiar issue. Their final significance
is that they simply carry on the central burden of the book, the frantic attempt
to know something of one another. Perversion is no single act; but rather,
any unaffecting love.

Baldwin has constructed his terrible dialectic; he has drawn up the battle
lines so that we may never be safe again. But what he has done, in scrupulously
avoiding everybody's social protest novel, is to write everybody's existential
novel. The problem is more than being fashionable. For one thing, as Ralph
Ellison has shown us, the Negro as a character has all the clichés of the existential
malady built-in. The absurdity of his status, the necessity of his rebellion, is
culturally given. He is defined as much by others' misconceptions of him as
by any self-perception, he is still what he always has been in our literature—
that most immediate example of God's default. Contemporary literature in
this respect is unique only in that it believes God was wrong.

This kind of status also has its uses. James's characters have an extraordinary
freedom based on money—and it is no accident that Baldwin's characters are
similarly unaffected by conventional economic problems. This is not because
they are more spiritual, but simply because this is as accurate an index of modern
affluent society as James's analysis of the international aristocracy. In short,
the economics of both situations are only manifestations of more significant
and complex problems. Rufus did not kill himself because he did not have
enough to eat when he was a child, but because he understood the dimensions
of ignorance and fear, one consequence of which was to affect his diet.
Unhampered by the obvious, Baldwin has cut through the pop-sociology of
his time to the roots of contemporary frustration—the curse not of slavery,
but leisure; not of organization, but alienation; not of social evil, but of individual love. Baldwin's assertion that we are all second-class citizens in our

existential dilemma, that the terms of our exclusion are similar, is his greatest achievement. In the end, his protagonists are not black anymore than we are white.

But such status may also be abused. For after self-consciousness, after all the billboards are down, then what? The message of this existentialism is the equality of guilt, the equality of men before no law – but when the rebellion has been justified, then what happens? Experience under these assumptions is predictable, sensibility has but one consequence. To say that the self is not what we commonly thought, even to say it again and again, is not to say what the self is.

"We have so completely debunked the old idea of the Self," Saul Bellow has said, "that we can hardly continue in the same way." And Baldwin cannot continue in the same way, if he is to further confront the problems he has set himself in *Another Country*.

Another Country is our country, real, repressed, and envisioned, and Baldwin's return to it does not break down the parallel with James in the least. His point of view remains that of the exile. Under existential assumptions, self-exile, to paraphrase a politician, is not a choice, but a condition. It is the condition of that *powerless, feeling young man*, an echo of that "reaction against a mistake," that dangling emasculate Negro, that rage to be "other almost anyhow."

But how do you differentiate when everybody is "other" anyway? Why do Rufus and Richard give up? Why do Ida and Vivaldo persevere? These are ambiguities in the work that cannot be justified by saying that life is ambiguous as well. The underground man is pretty thin fare by this time. Too many of us live there now to be celebrated as either indicative or unique. "There is no structure," Baldwin says, "that he [the artist] can build to keep out self-knowledge." But he has not yet demonstrated, except in his essays, that the artist can build a structure to *use* self-knowledge.

In this regard, he may profit once again from his mentor. For *Another Country* is as much a *vie en provence* as, say, *The Bostonians*. And both mark similar stages of maturity for their authors. Both books tend to abstract national character through a microcosm; an abstraction which can only be justified by elaboration in later work. It is a question of giving corroborative detail to a general observation, rather than letting the generalization, powerful as it may be, stand for the detail. For example, when James says of Miss Birdseye that "the whole moral history of Boston was reflected in her displaced spectacles," he is indulging himself in a sort of phrase which saves the book from the commonplace, but commits the author eventually to a more subtle analysis.

With this in mind, consider this paragraph from *Another Country*:

> Rufus walked, one of the fallen—for the weight of the city was
> murderous—one of those who had been crushed on the day, which
> was every day, these towers fall. Entirely alone and dying of it,
> he was part of an unprecedented multitude . . . that could scarcely
> bear their knowledge.

Moral histories ought to be exemplified, not simply invoked. It is the individual
who defines the multitude, not the other way around.

Although James's personal conflicts do not seem as compelling (modern)
as Baldwin's, he was certainly faulted for the same sort of abstraction. Eliot
maintained that he failed to "detect his own characters." Gide spoke of his
personages as "winged busts." Edmund Wilson at one time was moved to
proclaim that Hyacinth Robinson of the *Princess Casamassima* died of "the class
struggle," but F. W. Dupee is more to the point in stating that he died of a
"poverty of ideas." What he means is that Hyacinth is without the insight to
sustain himself as a character. His impotence is as unexamined as Rufus's appetite.
They are too good for the world and too abstract for literature.

Yet James refused to be satisfied by the type of the *powerless, feeling young
man*, for he knew how easy it was for him to uphold such a one, and how
graciously his audience would accept him. He was too involved in his own
cultural adventure to settle for the drama of limited character and obvious
dichotomy. His concern can be seen in his notebooks—"the web of
consciousness," his own metaphor, replaces the dialectic as a structural principle.
Whatever the argument over the convolutions of the later style, the consequences
of his continued exile, it is apparent that the later heroes of sensibility are
transfigured, and again I use his own words, into "personalities of transcendent
value." He is not satisfied simply to doom his characters in his later work,
not because they ought not to go down, but because that story was written—
those conflicts were charted—and now the problem was to develop the internal
relations between the sides he had so artfully chosen. It was a question of creating
characters sufficiently complex to sustain them beyond the dialectical conflict
which created them.

The turning point in James's career was perhaps *The Ambassadors*, in which
Strether renounces his cautiousness in the famous exhortation, "Get all the
experience you can." This does not refer to a more romantic life-style; it is
more like the Turgenev character in *Virgin Soil* who says "I could not simplify
myself." As usual, James reinforces this character's particular dialogue with an
unspoken generalization, "it was the proportions that were changed, and
the proportions were at all times, he philosophized, the very conditions of

perception, the terms of thought." The remarkable thing about these later characters is that they refuse to draw conclusions that would preclude further investigation on their part, and for that matter, further involvement for the reader. The galling thing about Baldwin's characters—and most "existential" heroes—is that they are so susceptible to conclusions which define them immediately. It is not that their truth is bitter, it is that their truth comes so easily—however hard it may be to shake it. In fact, they are all *ficelles*.

The quality of the later James lies in the tension between characters. Who is guilty? Who is innocent? Our final knowledge is that Paris, France, and Wollett, Mass., are not knowable without the other, that the categories with which we began the book no longer can apply. Radical innocence and guileless evil are neither opposed nor reconciled—they are intermeshed in a genuine mystery. Baldwin is shocking; not yet terrifying. What he has shown us is that everyone is guilty. This is the true paradox of the existential hero, for in all his hefty insistence that rebellion is justified, he seems to end up lacking the energy to achieve the *engagement* to which he pays his coffeehouse lip service.

Henry James was able to achieve what his notebooks anticipated: the reclamation of large areas of social experience, the transformation of these abstractions into material for the imagination. Baldwin has yet to progress beyond the initial encounter. He has, most powerfully, given us an opportunity to test our preconceptions, but that ultimately is social science, not literature.

The question remains, why pick on Baldwin when these are questions to be applied to modern fiction generally? Why does he take the burden of the breakthrough?

For one thing, Baldwin has progressed in each of his works, his dialectic has become progressively more refined. He has shown a flexibility and perseverance equal to our most influential artists. Further, and almost alone, he has continued to confront the unmanageable questions of modern society, rather than creating a nuclear family in which semantic fantasies may be enacted with no reference to the larger world except that it stinks. There can be no escape into technique or historiography. It will not do for him to remember something else. He must continue to find out about himself. It is his actual experience, perhaps, even more than the shaping of it, which will be crucial. To bring us to the door in Rufus's name will not be enough next time.

Baldwin's experience is unique among our artists in that his artistic achievements mesh so precisely with his historical circumstances. He is that nostalgic type—an artist speaking for a genuinely visible revolution. He is first in line for that Nirvana of American liberals, a Ministry of Culture. As with James, his problem is to give artistic life to the critical insights of his prefaces, his notebooks, in short, to develop characters which have a subtle and various consciousness equal to the omniscient, cranky narrator of the essays. This particular problem accounts for the failure of both artists as playwrights. Theatrical success depends upon rendering the particulars of a character through bald dialogue. Only rarely can a narrator amplify a character through abstract description; no disembodied voice can bridge the gap between an idea and its personification as in an essay or narrative literature. For those obsessed with the dialectic, for those whose characters are forever battling their own abstraction, the proscenium marks a treacherous zone.

Yet the very critical faculties which confine a sensibility may liberate it in the long run. Baldwin knows more than he has yet translated into literature. Like his mentor, he has used the essay, not as exposition in lieu of a work of larger intent, but as a testing ground for his fiction. Consider these notes of a native son:

> I could not be certain whether I was really rich or really poor, really black or really white, really male or really female, really talented or a fraud, really strong or merely stubborn. In short, I had become an American.

> At that time it seemed only too clear that love had gone out of the world, and not, as I had thought once, because I was poor and ugly and obscure, but precisely because I was no longer any of these things.

These remarkable observations are a fit foundation for Baldwin's future development.

Critics are at their most useless when they try to second-guess the proper conditions of an artist's experience, but is it too much to suggest that an American artist can finally make use of his notoriety? Is it not possible that the invasions of his privacy, the mass meetings, the TV appearance, the form letters, the suspicion of his protégés, the galling affection of his enemies, cannot provide a further insight into our society? Baldwin has had his winter of a hundred dinner parties. "Try to be one of those," James says, "upon whom nothing is lost." What happens when a poet becomes an acknowledged legislator? What happens to the rebel who finds that the price of one's resistance is that one has no reality beyond the resistance? That has always been the paradox of our rebels, and it has never been explored. And does not this paradox speak to our condition more than any ritualistic homage to the absurd? Is not the real "existential" dilemma that of this sensitive man who is never alone, engaged even against his will, whose paradox lies in his very power?

"The moral is that the flower of art blooms only where the soil is deep, that . . ." it takes a great deal of literature to produce a little history, that it needs a complex writer to set a social machinery in motion.

EDWARD MARGOLIES

The Negro Church: James Baldwin and the Christian Vision

One of the few cultural institutions the Southern Negro transplanted to Northern soil with a modicum of success was his church. Initially its principal purpose was to serve the spiritual needs of the community, but as time went on the Church came to function as a kind of community newspaper linking the new migrants to their Southern past. In this respect the importance of the ghetto churches cannot be overestimated.

Migration to the cities constituted the most abrupt break in the Negro cultural experience since the days of the African slave trade. It was not simply the anxieties of the passage from a rural to an urban way of life—these, after all, were the afflictions of most Eastern and Central European immigrants around the turn of the century—it was more that the racial mores, prejudices, and barriers of the North were ill-defined, vague, and elusive so that the Negro felt he stood on ever-shifting grounds whose pitfalls were at once invisible and treacherous. Negro votes were courted in some parts of the country and discouraged in others. In New York, service trades such as barbering and catering, which at one time had been the almost exclusive province of Negroes, seemed suddenly to pass out of their hands and become the domain of Caucasian foreigners, while neighborhoods such as Greenwich Village, the Hell's Kitchen area, and the mid-Sixties of the West Side were suddenly theirs and almost as suddenly not, all in the passage of forty years or so after the Civil War. In the South, at least, a Negro knew where he stood, however barren and bitter his place. Above all, there existed in the South a pattern of interpersonal relationships among whites and Negroes—rooted, to be sure, in racial pre-

From *Native Sons: A Critical Study of Twentieth-Century Black American Authors.* © 1968 by Edward Margolies. J. B. Lippincott Co., 1968.

conceptions, but for all that occasionally warm and recognizable—so closely interwoven had been the lives of both races over the centuries. But the white Northerner, when he was not downright hostile, treated Negroes with cold and faceless indifference. If he granted them greater self-expression, he seemed at the same time to be saying, "You may amuse me from time to time with your quaint and primitive antics, but in all significant areas of my life please keep away." For the Southern Negro migrant, the emotional stresses must have been intolerable.

It was precisely in this area that the Negro church functioned so effectively as an integrative force. It connected the Southern Negro with his former life, and gave him a socially acceptable outlet for his rage, his terror, and his frustrations—in its thinly veiled apocalyptic warnings, its evangelical fervor, and its promises of a better life to come. It also functioned as a political force, drawing together persons of diverse Southern origin and directing them toward goals which did not seem threatening to the established white power structure. Negro ministers were approached by white politicians who requested their support in elections, in return for favors to their communities and especially to themselves. This afforded the more successful Negro clergy—those with large congregations—some bargaining power. It never amounted to much, the way the world reckons these affairs, but it did provide a foothold of sorts in the great world beyond the ghetto.

The pluralistic and anarchic aspects of city life wrought their disintegrative forces on the Negro church just as they did on churches outside the Negro community. First-and second-generation urban Negroes tend, on the whole, to look less and less to evangelical Christianity as the source of their spiritual and emotional salvation. Still, the Messianic strain, the apocalyptic vision, the imagery and the fervor of the church, live on in the Negro community, fashioned now to more material and worldly ends. Indeed, the transfer of religious energies to political and social causes has swept along many Negro clergymen into what has since been called the Negro Revolt. The spirit of evangelism still permeates all areas of Negro culture.

Nowhere has this been so apparent as in the works of James Baldwin. In a sense, Baldwin is himself a symbol of this change. He was born in Harlem in 1924, the stepson of an evangelical minister, and was brought up in an atmosphere suffused with piety and puritanical rigor. His stepfather, stern, distant and authoritarian, insisted that his children devote as much spare time as they could to his views of Christian teachings. The evangelical church demanded much of the emotional and intellectual energies of its members, and it is a measure of Baldwin's commitment that he became a Young Minister at the age of fourteen. Baldwin's Christian ardor began to cool in favor of literature when he attended high school, but his writing career has been shaped by the rhetoric of evangelism and by his childhood understanding of the nature of the Christian's experience.

Underlying the American experience, there persists to this day a strain of sheer Utopianism. Implicit in this vision is the notion of the goodness and purity of innocence as opposed to the evil of experience. The paradox lies of course in the fact that as Americans exercise themselves to recapture their innocence, they become more and more contaminated by their experience. This is one of the major themes of American letters. In a peculiar sort of way, Baldwin is at once the captive of this vision and, by virtue of his alienated status as a Negro, outside of it. Baldwin speaks everywhere of the "monstrous heart," the dark secrets of the soul—sinister and complex passions, the realities of which white Americans (as opposed to Europeans) refuse to recognize. As a Negro and a homosexual (hence doubly an outsider), against whom dreadful injustices have been perpetrated, he is particularly sensitive to this idea. And yet in his fiction, it is not the heart that destroys and betrays his protagonists, but what happens to innocence when the heart confronts the cruelly corrupt world. Thus Baldwin's characters generally end up more outraged and submerged than they began. But being true Americans, they continue to strive for what they know must ultimately defeat them.

This is not to suggest that the struggle against oppression and injustice is futile or undesirable, but rather that Baldwin does not recognize in himself the same failing of which he accuses white Americans: the inability to see that evil exists, that it is just as much an indelible portion of existence as is oxygen in the air. Were his characters to come to terms with their own hearts, they might be better able to survive. But this is asking for a level of maturity that few American authors have ever been able to achieve.

The only salvation Baldwin seems willing to offer in concrete or specific terms is the homosexual experience (in his latest novel, *Another Country*, 1962), but here Baldwin has retreated so far from the experiential world that the "truth" he has discovered is scarcely adequate. The homosexual theme is not unrelated to the kind of evangelical orientation Baldwin brings to his novels. What obscures the connection is Baldwin's own special relationship to his stepfather. In his essays, he writes that his stepfather was mean and distrustful and would not allow his children to get close to him. Baldwin's fiction, too, is replete with characters who are unable to establish relationships with their fathers, and who consequently reach out to other males for the kind of masculine love they were denied as children.

But even beyond the question of sexual development, there exists the problem of personal identity in a male-dominated society which only a father image can provide. The high proportion of fatherless Negro lower-class families has been noted many times by Negro authors and sociologists and psychologists generally. The sense of masculine identity is a very real problem for growing Negro boys. Add to this the emasculating effects of a white society that debases Negro men as clowns or "boys" and denies them the kind of meaningful work in which they could take pride.

The Negro church partially fulfills their psychic needs. By identifying themselves with a strong and wrathful Old Testament God, they assume vicariously the masculinity they have missed in their family and social lives. But in order for them to come to Him, they must abase themselves before Him, reject and condemn their worldly and sensual impulses and passively await the insemination of His divine spirit and grace. They thus become, momentarily at least, female in their quest for the masculinity that would provide them with identity. This becomes especially clear in the case of Baldwin, whose sexual and emotional development was stunted by an unloving father and an unresponsive society; evangelical Christianity provided him with some sort of psychic compensation.

Baldwin is, of course, aware of the latent sexual components of the religious experience. In one of his early short stories, "The Outing" (1951), he employs the setting of a church boat trip along the Hudson to describe an adolescent's efforts to achieve the love and security of a male companion after his father has publicly humiliated him. Johnnie's pathos is reflected in the service that takes place in the great hall of the boat, when the congregation cries out passionately for the strength and guidance of their God.

> Yet, in the copper sunlight Johnnie felt suddenly, not the presence of the Lord, but the presence of David; which seemed to reach out to him, hand reaching out to hand in the fury of flood-time, to drag him to the bottom of the water or to carry him safe to shore. From the corner of his eye he watched his friend, who held him with such power; and felt, for that moment, such a depth of love, such nameless and terrible joy and pain, that he might have fallen, in the face of that company, weeping at David's feet.

Baldwin's other stories do not use a specifically religious context, but the evangelical element is seldom very far distant. Characters sing or hum snatches of hymns as they go about their daily round of frustrations, and in at least two of the stories, "Sonny's Blues" (1957) and "Going to Meet the Man" (1965), a kind of ritual quality lurks in the very essence of the narrative.

"Sonny's Blues" is the story of a jazz pianist who seeks a means for expressing the grief and terror that rage within his soul. The story is told by Sonny's brother, a high-school teacher, who fears that Sonny may begin anew an addiction to heroin from which, ostensibly, he has just been cured. The climax of the story is reached when Sonny happens upon some evangelists "testifying" on a street corner. Later Sonny proceeds to a nightclub in Greenwich Village where he hopes to renew his career as a musician. After a few halting starts, he finds his expression with the band. In a sense Sonny "testifies"—and the musicians and his audience are his witnesses.

> I had the feeling that, in a way, everyone on the bandstand was waiting for him, both waiting for him and pushing him along. But as I began to watch Creole, I realized that it was Creole who held them all back. He had them on a short rein. Up there, keeping the beat with his whole body, wailing on the fiddle, with his eyes half closed, he was listening to everything, but he was listening to Sonny. He was having a dialogue with Sonny. He wanted Sonny to leave the shoreline and strike out for the deep water. He was Sonny's witness that deep water and drowning were not the same thing—he had been there, and he knew.
>
> Freedom lurked around us and I understood, at last, that he could help us to be free if we would listen, that he would never be free until we did.

"Going to Meet the Man" is a unique story in the Baldwin repertoire because here for the only time in his fiction, he attempts to probe the mind of the violent oppressor. The story is related from the point of view of a middle-aged sheriff who has been brutally engaging civil rights demonstrators in a small Southern town. He tries to understand their persistence, but their defiance and hatred baffle him. After one especially grueling day, he attempts unsuccessfully to make love to his wife; he is weary and feels himself utterly depleted. His mind goes back to his childhood when his father and mother took him to a lynching at which seemingly the entire white community was present. The whole scene is vivid in his memory—the gouged and plucked eyes, the repeated dousing of gasoline on the naked black body as he was periodically lowered from a tree into the fire below, and finally the Negro's castration by one of the executioners with a butcher knife. The crowd—men and women alike—stares fascinated and thrilled at the spectacle. The memory of this event arouses in the sheriff a renewed desire for his wife. "Come on, sugar," he whispers to his wife, "I'm going to do you like a nigger, just like a nigger, come on, sugar, and love me just like you'd love a nigger."

The weird and macabre ritual evidently serves to relieve the townspeople of their own sexual fantasies and guilt. In punishing the Negro they have cleansed themselves, while at the same time they vicariously partake of his presumed potency. In effect Baldwin is saying that the white Southerner (and Northerner too for that matter) requires the Negro as a scapegoat for his sexual guilt and at the same time secretly desires him for his sexual power. It is interesting to note how Baldwin, even in this kind of extreme situation, discovers in his church-oriented psychology an understanding of his oppressors' behavior. Confession-expression, however enacted—symbolically in the lynching of the Negro, or among one's kindred spirits in a jazz club or a revival meeting— serves as a restorative of innate spiritual powers that have been depleted or atrophied by the experience of living in the mean void of the day-to-day world.

The prototypical church experience is related in Baldwin's first novel, *Go Tell It on the Mountain* (1953). Essentially it is the story of fourteen-year-old John Grimes's conversion, but the truly major figure of interest is John's father, Gabriel—and it is Gabriel, chiefly, around whom all the other characters' difficulties are centered. This is in a sense Baldwin's most ambitious book, in that he endeavors here not only to interconnect the lives and psychology of all the characters but also to relate these to the Southern Negro experience and the consequent shocks of urban slum living. The church, naturally, somewhat softens the impact—indeed makes their lives endurable, but it becomes clear in this novel that Baldwin regards the church as only a kind of temporary palliative and that dangerous trials lie ahead.

The novel is divided into three parts. The first part, "The Seventh Day," establishes the attitudes of John, his mother Elizabeth, and his Aunt Florence toward Gabriel—whom they alternately hate, fear, or distrust. Gabriel is a stern, aloof, self-righteous man with a scarcely concealed animosity toward John. He is a deacon of his church and commands his family in an imperious, hostile, arrogant manner. John is a sensitive, brooding boy, troubled with a sense of sin, distressed at his worldly desires, yearning guiltily to break free from the bounds of the ghetto into the exotic white world beyond. After a particularly dreadful scene with his father in which the whole family participates, he goes to the family church to perform some janitorial duties in preparation for the Saturday night "tarry" services. Here he meets Elisha, a seventeen-year-old Young Minister. John feels a strange physical attraction toward Elisha, and they tussle playfully. Later, several of the elders of the Church—the Saints, as they call themselves—enter to sing and worship and contemplate their souls. As the section closes, John's mother, father, and aunt join them.

The tone of "The Seventh Day" is one of futility, of unyielding frustration that permeates the lives of all the characters, indeed of the Harlem community itself—and the reader is made to feel that they and their posterity are doomed to an existence of shabby poverty and soured dreams. A significant passage details John's household chores. His mother has asked him to clean the rug and John thinks of Sisyphus pushing his boulder up the hill.

> He had John's entire sympathy, for the longest and hardest part of his Saturday mornings was his voyage with the broom across this endless rug; and, coming to the French doors that ended the living room and stopped the rug, he felt like an indescribably weary traveler who sees his home at last. Yet for each dustpan he so laboriously filled at the doorsill demons added to the rug twenty more; he saw in the expanse behind him the dust that he had raised settling again into the carpet; and he gritted his teeth, already on edge because of the dust that filled his mouth, and nearly wept to think that so much labor brought so little reward.

The narrowness of their lives compels each character to seize his identity where he may, however senseless and self-defeating it may appear. Thus Gabriel maintains an authoritarian righteousness as head of his family even though he knows that his lack of charity has alienated him from their love. John cherishes his intelligence and his hatred of his father as being his own unique identity, and longs for the time he can emulate the white actress he had seen in a film that very day, who seemed to be telling the entire appalled and nasty world it could go to hell. But John knows in his heart that it is a fantasy, and that in some profound and mysterious way over which he has had no control, his fate has been long settled.

The stage has been thus set to examine the lives of Florence, Gabriel, and Elizabeth, in whom the seeds of John's fate are buried. In the second part of the novel, "The Prayers of the Saints," the three are seen at their prayers, each seeking the causes of his misery as he wanders back and forth over memories of the past.

It develops that Gabriel and Florence were brought up in the deep South by a pious mother whose other children had been taken from her during the bitter days of slavery. Despite their mother's constant prayers for their salvation, both Gabriel and Florence rejected her in her lifetime — Florence seeking a better life for herself in the North, while Gabriel stayed behind, sunk deep in sin, whisky, and disreputable women. Florence eventually married in the North, but her attempts to elevate her husband to bourgeois status failed utterly — and he left her for another woman, declaring that he wanted to remain the kind of common "nigger" she despised. Gabriel, meanwhile, experienced a religious conversion after his mother's death, and shortly thereafter became a preacher whose renown spread quickly throughout the region. He married a plain, sickly woman, Deborah, who bore him no children—a disappointment that bitterly rankled. At the height of his fame and despite himself, he had a brief liaison with a younger woman, Esther, whom he afterwards sent away when she told him she was going to have his baby. Esther died after the birth of their son, Royal, but Royal was brought up in Gabriel's town, and Gabriel silently watched him grow into a cocky and arrogant young man. Just prior to her own death, Deborah tells her husband that Royal has been murdered in Chicago, and that she has always suspected Gabriel of being his father. Her dying words to Gabriel are that he had better repent.

Elizabeth met Florence when they both worked as scrubwomen in a downtown New York office building. Elizabeth, too, had suffered a severe, puritanical upbringing, under the guardianship of an unloving aunt in Maryland. When she was nineteen she came north to Harlem, following a young man with whom she had fallen in love. Richard, sensitive, tormented, and angrily bitter at the white world, committed suicide, ignorant of the fact that he had sired her baby. Florence introduced Elizabeth to Gabriel after the latter had come North following the death of his wife. Gabriel, evidently desiring to atone for his neglect of Esther and Royal, regarded the unwed Elizabeth and her infant, John, as a kind of second chance God had revealed to him. But Gabriel is uncapable of giving Elizabeth and John the kind of love and protection they need. He is too full of his own sense of cosmic importance, and lavishes all ardor on his own blood son, Roy (Elizabeth has borne him three other children as well), whom he regards as being part of God's strange designs.

Florence, in turn, has hated Gabriel since childhood. It was she who had been ambitious and desired an education to improve herself, but her mother unaccountably devoted all her attention to Gabriel, whose worthlessness and selfishness were patently obvious to all. It is interesting to note that Florence attempted to manage her husband in much the same way her mother had attempted to manage Gabriel—and, like her mother, failed utterly. Florence cannot understand where she was mistaken. She has endeavored to emulate the middle-class life, but the results are quite the same as if she had never tried. She is old and alone now, living in abject poverty in a miserable Harlem room. Her greatest residual passion is simply to inflict pain on Gabriel, whom she blames for all her wretchedness. She wants as well to protect Elizabeth, whose marriage to Gabriel she feels partially responsible for.

It is clear, then, that the prayers of the Saints are not quite so spiritual as one might expect, but Baldwin, with nice irony, suggests that prayer is the only thing they have. And underlying their prayer is an immense anger, scarcely concealed, at a universe that has suppressed and choked them.

Part 3, "The Threshing Floor," is once more John's story. Falling prey unconsciously to a variety of emotions, John suddenly experiences a lengthy religious conversion, flinging himself prone on the floor of the church. It clearly festers in Gabriel that his bastard stepson—and not one of his own blood decendants—is now one of the elect. Florence, sensing her brother's bitterness toward John, threatens to reveal the contents of a letter that Deborah had sent her just before she died, which tells of Gabriel's dalliance with Esther and his subsequent neglect of his illegitimate son. Florence hopes, in so doing, to exact revenge on the brother she has hated all her life. John feels immense and mysterious forces at work in his life, and in an intensely passionate scene at the end of the service, he asks Elisha to remember him at these moments of his splendor regardless of what may happen to him in later years.

Each of the actors in Baldwin's drama has thus somehow "ritualized" the dominant passions of his life in the externals of religious worship. Gabriel remains embittered and righteous, Florence hating and wretched, Elizabeth bewildered and tormented, and it is suggested that John has now discovered and recognized his homosexuality. Religion has not liberated them from themselves permanently, but it has "objectified" their misery momentarily, and so has helped them to survive. This is especially true of John, whose fear and guilt and desire and despair and hatred have all been converted into a kind of meaningful delirium as he lies thrashing about the floor.

Ordinarily revelations of this nature produce an ability to cope better with the tragic conditions of one's life; an enhanced self-awareness implies an enhanced possibility of human action to adjust to the conditions of existence. But unfortunately for Baldwin's characters, they are as utterly hopeless at the end of the novel as at the beginning. This is their private hell—and perhaps the Negro's; they know but they cannot act. From time to time their misery will be alleviated in the communal act of prayer but ultimately their despair is immovable. And one's final impression is of Baldwin's characters frozen in tableaux, arrested in prayer while a host of furies play about their heads and hearts.

In subsequent novels, Baldwin makes use of his church-oriented psychology in areas of subject matter one would not ordinarily expect. *Giovanni's Room* (1956) relates an American white youth's discovery of himself in the arms of his male lover, a tormented Italian bartender in Paris in the years shortly after World War II. David, who had been planning to marry, gives up his Giovanni when his fiancée comes to Paris. The engaged couple go to the south of France, where they live together for a while, but David cannot escape thoughts of Giovanni. His guilt is exacerbated by the knowledge that since he rejected him, the tender Giovanni has degenerated into a tramp among Paris pederasts, and has committed murder in a final act of desperation. David learns through the newspapers that Giovanni has been apprehended, tried, and found guilty, and is about to be executed. Shortly after Giovanni's death, David leaves Hella, his fiancée, whom he now finds physically revolting, and consorts for several days with homosexuals whom he picks up in bars on the Riviera. Hella finds him one night, and her new knowledge of her lover constrains her to break their engagement and return to America. The novel ends as David prepares to go back to Paris—doomed, he now knows, to suffer the endless rebuffs, humiliations, and torments of a homosexual.

The novel suffers on several scores, not the least of which is an absence of character growth or discernment. Hella is portrayed as a bright but stereotypically shallow and neurotic American girl, devoid of the kind of passion and sensitivity David has found in Giovanni. Giovanni, on the other hand, is a wraithlike, childlike figure, who demands David's total love and attention. Aside from a few of the usual acid remarks about America and Americans that one has come to expect from sensitive foreigners in expatriate novels, Giovanni reveals scarcely any of the insight or depth of feeling that Baldwin attributes to him. The best that one can say here is that this is a recognition novel—David discovers that he is a homosexual (something that the reader could have told him on page three), and that he feels sorry for himself that he has discovered this dreadful knowledge. Even so, one suspects that David delights in his newborn sorrow and that in order to indulge it he has unconsciously manipulated the hapless Giovanni and the lonely, aggressive American girl.

The novel is not without its virtues. There is a certain economy—something suggestive of Poe, not only in narrative quality (the first person confessional of the dark and sinister ways of the heart), but in the overwhelming suggestion of horror that suffuses the atmosphere. If the ultimate horror proves itself not very horrible, Baldwin does manage some very good scenes that shriek with a kind of terror. Early in the novel he describes in macabre detail the homosexual bar in which David first meets Giovanni. Here the lowlife of the homosexual community congregates nightly—the male prostitutes and their aging wealthy patrons, the streetwalkers, the pimps, the near transvestites. Gathered together, gossiping, flirting, giggling in the unreal light of the bar, they suggest something of the demons in a Bosch painting. Baldwin's description of Giovanni's sordid and claustrophobic room—where David and Giovanni pass some of their most idyllic moments—is almost surrealistically rendered as the evil world which engulfs their innocence. But beyond the particular successes and failures of the novel are the ways in which Baldwin has transmogrified his Christian vision into the ostensibly revolutionary subject matter of his novel.

Christian love has here been transfigured into masculine love, the one redeeming grace in Baldwin's neo-Calvinist vision of a corrupt and depraved world. David's failure is that he has failed to "bear witness" to Giovanni's suffering—that he has failed to give him the love Giovanni demanded in order that he might survive. There follows then a curiously ambivalent attitude about the nature of human experience and of the human body. On the one hand, the world and experience become somehow the equivalent of the body, in that all three are viewed as the corruptive elements of the original purity of the soul. Giovanni and David cry out on more than one occasion about the vileness of their bodies and the world. Not surprisingly, this revulsion is directed more toward women than men, although Giovanni's homosexual bar appears as an inversion of paradise. Yet the female, Hella, is not inappropriately named either, in view of the pain David suffers when he is alone with her, in contrast to the heaven he knows with Giovanni.

On the other hand, the body and worldly experience, properly understood, are instruments of grace. This is something Giovanni knows by intuition, but which David has learned too late. The violation of innocence (or goodness), sad as this may be, is not totally evil, for it may lend depth to one's humanity. It is the religious paradox of good issuing from evil. But here innocence is discovered in the relationship of men who have not yet been contaminated with the notion of love as being exclusively heterosexual. For Baldwin it is only in homosexual love that innocence is experienced anew. The implication here is that innocence first existed in prepubescent youth. Giovanni, for all his worldly wisdom, is a child, a "baby," a "boy." David resents and simultaneously delights in mothering him. To David, the greatest pathos is in children whose innocence must one day be transgressed—by worldly experience—as was his.

> The city, Paris, which I loved so much was absolutely silent.
> . . . Behind the walls of the houses I passed, the French nation was
> clearing away the dishes, putting little Jean Pierre and Marie to
> bed. . . . Those walls, those shuttered windows held them in and
> protected them against the darkness and the long moan of this long
> night. Ten years hence, little Jean Pierre or Marie might find
> themselves out here beside the river and wonder, like me, how they
> had fallen out of the web of safety. What a long way, I thought,
> I've come—to be destroyed.

David's love affair with Giovanni exists outside chronological time—within the womb, as it were, at the beginning of creation.

> I remember that life in that room seemed to be occurring beneath
> the sea. Time flowed past indifferently above us; hours and days

had no meaning. In the beginning, our life together held a joy and
amazement which was newborn every day.

Baldwin depicts David's innocent beginning with Giovanni as an Old Testament
Eden, the remembrance of which leaves him maddened with melancholy. He
invokes further biblical imagery when he describes David's torment over whether
or not to tell Giovanni he is leaving.

> I moved toward him as though I were driven, putting my hands
> on his shoulders and forcing myself to look into his eyes. I smiled
> and I really felt at that moment that Judas and the Savior had met
> in me.

But if David's desertion of Giovanni is, in the last analysis, indefensible,
it is also inevitable, because David is an American, whose civilization has taught
him to deny the existence of pain and suffering and death. And it is precisely
because he evades these realities that he is unable to accept the Eden Giovanni
offers him, for Baldwin believes it is impossible for the adult to recapture his
innocence until he accepts the tragedy of existence.

All of which leads Baldwin to describe another kind of innocence — one
antithetical to Giovanni's — an American innocence, carefully designed to ignore
the terrors that afflict the human heart by the simple refusal to admit their
possibilities. In effect this kind of innocence is evil, because it fails to allow
the full potentialities of human life, and thereby deprives persons of the full
measure of their sex and individuality, and it leads to the most brutal kinds
of racism, denying the humanity of others. Thus Baldwin equates sexual and
racial intolerance as deriving from the same kind of mentality.

In *Another Country* (1962), Baldwin assumes an increasingly militant tone,
focusing on the superiority of the Negro and the homosexual by virtue of their
extended suffering. The homosexual and Negro are shown as one in that they
have both gleaned the value of suffering and are thus both redeemable. The
average white American, on the other hand, because he has submerged a
knowledge of himself, dwells in a kind of psychic hell.

Indeed here Baldwin's America (mainly Greenwich Village) is almost a
literal hell in the oppressive heat of a New York summer. The plot is much
too complicated to rehearse here in its entirety. There is no one central character, but the most sympathetic figure is a white homosexual actor named Eric,
who returns from France and, in the course of events, sleeps with an unhappily
married woman (Cass) and with the distressed white lover (Vivaldo) of a Negro
girl (Ida), thereby introducing them to the mysteries of the human heart. Eric,
however, remains true in his fashion to Yves, a young Frenchman with whom

he had been living idyllically in France. At the end of the novel Yves flies to America to rejoin Eric in New York, the implication being that the two lovers reborn in their love will fashion a new heaven out of the hell of America.

The most intriguing character in the novel is Rufus, Ida's brother, whom Baldwin unfortunately kills off by suicide early in the book. It is Rufus's ghost that haunts all of the other major characters—indeed brings them together. Rufus, a jazz musician, had fallen in love with a white Southern girl, but the social and psychological pressures of living with Leona had so riven him that he killed himself. The people who knew and loved Rufus are made partly responsible for his death, although precisely where their responsibility lies is never quite made clear. Obviously they did not understand the extent of Rufus's suffering and hence were unable to bear witness—but, being white, they *could* not understand. And even if one were to grant the moral lassitude Baldwin attributes to them—and possibly some kind of a case might be made—the author lets them off much too easily. Vivaldo and Cass, for example, are awakened to a deeper understanding by sleeping with Eric. They are now presumably far more aware of the human condition—and especially the plight of the Negro. The homosexual experience is especially applicable to Vivaldo, who is undergoing a distressing relationship with his Negro mistress. Yet the reader is at pains to discover what magical properties Eric possesses. He is patient and forbearing and has yielded himself to countless lonely men who have clandestinely sought him out for the love they could find nowhere else, but he appears an amiable nondescript fellow. One wonders whether a heterosexual with the same generous qualities might not do the trick as well. But of course Baldwin's point is that a heterosexual is psychically ill-equipped to cope with loneliness, despair, and suffering—if he is white.

Rufus and Ida are in some respects the counterparts to Eric, for they live the dark and mysterious ways of the human spirit. Rufus dies because he has found no one to whom he could unburden his heart, but Ida, really an extension of her brother, is made of stronger stuff. Her most consuming passion is a rage at whites, because they are blind to the possibilities of their humanity, and because they use their power to curb the Negro life force. Since they are thwarted in so many other areas of self-expression, Baldwin can only display his Negro characters' superior prowess in jazz and sex. In these latter activities, Rufus and Ida are magnificent, and regard most whites with contempt. Ida tells Vivaldo:

> I used to see the way white men watched me, like dogs. And
> I thought about what I could do to them. How I hated them, the
> way they looked, and the things they'd say, all dressed up in their

damn white skin and their clothes just so, and their little weak, white pricks jumping in their drawers. You could do any damn thing with them if you just led them along, because they wanted to do something dirty and they knew that you knew how. All black people knew that. Only, the polite ones didn't say dirty. They said real. I used to wonder what in the world they did in bed, white people I mean, between themselves, to get them so sick.

Like Eric, who has served so many lonely, desperate, and unloved men, Ida, and Negro women like her, cater to the sick and impassioned needs of white men. Their sex serves to alleviate—at least temporarily—the anguish and the agony of the spiritual pariahs. They are, in a sense, priests, confessors, witnesses whose sexuality endows them with mysterious healing qualities, and because they are privy to the secret life of their supplicants, they possess a hidden knowledge and power that in some respects terrify the very persons who fly to them for succor. The terror is then translated into oppression and persecution in order to compel them to continue to play out their role as healers in the diseased sexual fantasies of white persons.

It is precisely this that most enrages and embitters Ida and Baldwin's other Negro characters. They must suffer and stifle and die in the miserable ghettos of America in order to appease the sickened psychic innocence of whites. It is at this juncture that Baldwin moves away from his vision of the Negro as the suffering servant, the scapegoat who returns his oppressors' scorn with love—. to a view of the Negro fighting angrily, forcefully, vigorously for simple justice, for the assertion and sanctity of his humanity. It is here apparently that Baldwin (in this book, in any event) divides the roles of the Negro and the homosexual. Homosexuals like Eric, one feels, will persevere as figures of compassion upon whom the guilty and the stricken will unburden themselves. Negroes, however, must refuse to embody such a role in the future. The Negro and the homosexual thus assume two attributes of the godhead—the Negro representing justice, the homosexual, mercy.

But it must not be supposed that justice necessarily implies something harsh and vindictive. By asserting his claim to full humanity, the Negro may restore the white American to a truer, more childlike innocence. Ida shocks her white lover, Vivaldo, by reciting her affair with another white man. In effect she tells him frankly the bitter truths of being a Negro in a white world. Vivaldo, having just recently slept with Eric, is now prepared to accept reality on a much deeper level than he had previously allowed himself. He tells Ida he still loves her and they fall into one another's arms. Ida thus completes the process of stripping her lover of his American innocence.

Suddenly, he reached out and pulled her to him, trembling, with tears starting up behind his eyes, burning and blinding, and covered her face with kisses, which seemed to freeze as they fell. She clung to him; with a sigh she buried her face in his chest. There was nothing erotic in it; they were like two weary children. And it was she who was comforting him. Her long fingers stroked his back, and he began, slowly, with a horrible, strangling sound, to weep, for she was stroking his innocence out of him.

Another Country possesses its own raw and violent power. And yet for all its heartfelt emotions, the novel scarcely gets anywhere. Somehow, sex and love and a vague knowledge of the enormities of the human heart are not sufficient to resolve the immense social, psychological, and moral issues of racism and alienation that Baldwin poses. They may represent a start but certainly not an end.

And even here Baldwin's anger somewhat shrouds his art. His Negro characters all speak with the same voice (Baldwin's), and sometimes the same syntax. Even his white characters—with the exception of the formidable Eric—although recognizable types, do not possess any sharply defined individuality. For the most part they react passively to the terrible emotions of their Negro friends—and their motivations are pap.

In Baldwin's extended essay, *The Fire Next Time* (1963), and his play, *Blues for Mr. Charlie* (1964), the church militant advances at the expense of the church of love and forbearance. *The Fire Next Time* is an extremely moving piece. Baldwin begins by relating his early youth in Harlem and all the attendant hardships, despair, and frustration of the Negro community. He then describes the particular appeal of the Black Muslim movement for the Negro—Baldwin had had an audience with Elijah Muhammad at his home in Chicago—despite the obvious impossibilities of several of its specific doctrines. He concludes with some speculations regarding the future of the Negro and the future of America itself. The essay is hardly organized in any classic sense. Random thoughts enter into the picture, and Baldwin frequently resorts to personal anecdotes to give substance to his own views. In effect, the essay is a prolonged polemic against racism and an almost wholesale attack on the entire American civilization of which racism is merely symptomatic. "Why," asks Baldwin, "should I want to be integrated into a burning house?"

The Negro must endeavor to extricate himself, but Baldwin's sermon is something more than a declaration of Negro independence; it is a clear statement that the white man's salvation depends upon the Negro. Suppression of the Negro is equated with suppression of knowledge of the darkness from which men sprang and of the darkness of death—hence, the terror of knowledge of life.

> One is responsible to life: it is the small beacon in that terrifying
> darkness from which we come and to which we shall return. One
> must negotiate this passage as nobly as possible, for the sake of those
> who are coming after us. But white Americans do not believe in
> death, and this is why the darkness of my skin so intimidates them.

But the Negro who has survived in white America has always been aware
of the precariousness of his life, and therefore knows its value and meaning.

> That man who is forced each day to snatch his manhood, his
> identity, out of the fire of human cruelty that rages to destroy it,
> knows, if he survives his effort, and even if he does not survive
> it, something about himself and human life that no school on
> earth—and indeed, no church—can teach.

The white man, if he is to become himself, must recognize the humanity of
the Negro, and he must recognize that he has projected on the Negro his own
fears and longings.

> The only way [the white man] can be released from the Negro's
> tyrannical power is to consent, in effect, to become black himself,
> to become a part of that suffering and dancing country that he now
> watches wistfully from the heights of his lonely power and, armed
> with spiritual traveler's checks, visits surreptitiously after dark.

To Baldwin, it is the height of absurdity and self-delusion for the white man
to assume the Negro wants to be his "equal." Indeed, quite the opposite: it
is the white man who must strive to learn from the Negro.

> Why, for example—especially knowing the family as I do—I should
> *want* to marry your sister is a great mystery to me. But your sister
> and I have every right to marry if we wish to. . . . If she cannot
> raise me to her level, perhaps I can raise her to mine.

There is a considerable difference between Baldwin and previous generations
of Negro polemicists who railed against the race-supremacy beliefs of white
Americans. Baldwin assumes the superiority of Negroes (not genetically, but
by virtue of their American experience, their suffering) and pleads for the equality
of *white* Americans. And though here and there he prescribes love and mutual
understanding, the tone is largely one of outrage. Baldwin warns that if his
prescription goes unheeded, the holocaust may be closer than most Americans
care to imagine.

In *Blues for Mr. Charlie*, Baldwin translates his apocalypse into concrete social terms. The race war is not yet quite upon us, but the play ends with preparation for a Negro protest march in a small Southern town in which its leader-minister keeps a gun in readiness concealed under his Bible. The alternatives are clear: love or violence, the Negro can wait no longer. Baldwin's theater resembles nothing so much—in form and fervor, at least—as the protest dramas of the radical left in the thirties. But the play is effective, for the emotions it arouses are specifically vindictive and personally embarrassing to his white audiences, which partly explains, no doubt, its failure on the Broadway stage. For Baldwin, the preacher, not only thunders at his audience's failure of social and human responsibility, but, far worse, he impugns their sexuality and depicts them as more terrified of the possibilities of life than the Negroes they persecute.

If the bare outline of the plot appears somewhat hackneyed, this perhaps only proves that Baldwin can work over old material with considerable skill. Related in flashbacks and in swift scenes with the stage occasionally divided between backdrops of the Negro and white communities, the play deals with the murder of Richard, a young man who has returned South after having flourished as a musician on the Harlem stage. He is recovering from dope addiction, and is thoroughly embittered at the life he met in the North. In the course of events, Richard taunts and insults the wife of Lyle, a white storekeeper, and when Richard refuses to apologize, Lyle shoots him. There is a trial, and of course the white jury exonerates Lyle. The tense atmosphere is aggravated by the fact that the town's Negroes have recently been demonstrating for their civil rights. Parnell, a rich newspaper publisher, is divided in loyalty between Lyle, a lifelong friend whose guilt he is afraid to acknowledge, and Meridian, Richard's father, who leads the civil rights marchers. In addition, Parnell is secretly in love with Juanita, a Negro girl, who has always loved Richard. In the end, he opts to align himself with the Negroes, but though he is allowed to march in the same direction, they do not yet accept him as one of them.

Oddly, Baldwin has been accused of simplifying issues and persons, when in actuality he has done quite the opposite. Richard, who nurtures his being in hate, is presented as highly neurotic, obstreperous, and disagreeable, and perhaps unconsciously invites his own death. His heroism—if that is what it may be called—lies in his ability to articulate all the venom and bitterness he feels toward whites. It is an act of courage, but there is little else about him that is admirable. On the other hand, Lyle, the murderer, is portrayed compassionately, almost sympathetically. His entire identity requires that he believe himself superior to Negroes. This, moreover, is related to his heated animal attraction to Negro women as opposed to his warped and repressed sexual feelings toward his wife. Finally, there can be little doubt that Richard has taunted and challenged him almost beyond forbearance. Curiously, here and in the short story, "Going to Meet the Man," Baldwin draws his white Southern racists more believably than he does his white Northern liberals.

What presumably disturbed the critics, however—although none of them admitted it—was Baldwin's implication that whites generally, liberals and racists alike, are varying versions of Lyle. Parnell, for example, a decent and respectable fellow with whom liberals might identify, dreams of reaching out to the black nation just beyond his reach—and describes his own world as a dull gray envelope. Similarly, the other white characters are revealed in their day-to-day activities not as mean, but as devitalized. The Negroes, on the other hand, express depths of passion as they debate the courses of action they must take in their struggle.

The point, however, is not psychological but moral. Given even the "worst kind" of Negro (Richard), and the most understandably provoked white man (Lyle), Baldwin is saying that simple justice demands the recognition of Negro humanity. The history that has produced Richard must never again be tolerated—even at the cost of violence. And it is fitting that Richard's father, a man of God, should say as the play ends, "You know, for us, it all began with the Bible and the gun. Maybe it will end with the Bible and the gun. . . . Like the pilgrims of old." Thus the steps from love to militancy are about to be taken, and a new history begins.

As an indictment of the sexual roots of racism, *Blues for Mr. Charlie* is sweeping. It is a propaganda piece with "real-life" characters—a rare achievement in protest drama. But the tentacles of the problem reach beyond society and sex into history, politics, and economics. Perhaps what is called for is surrealist-allegorical theater on the order of Genet's *The Blacks*. For racism—whatever else it is—is absurd, and it requires a more imaginative approach than Baldwin's Christian-Freudian interpretation.

What is encouraging is the new-found virility in Baldwin's prose. He recognizes the virtues of rage as well as its evils. And yet there are dangers as well. That Baldwin has the craftsman's way with words, there can be little doubt. As an essayist and polemicist he has few equals. But one wonders whether, as an artist, he may not now possibly consume himself in his recently recovered Jehovah-like rage.

ROGER ROSENBLATT

Out of Control: Go Tell It on the Mountain *and* Another Country

Go Tell It on the Mountain

The cyclical damnation which Baldwin depicts in *Go Tell It on the Mountain* is less sensational and picturesque than [Richard] Wright's [in *Native Son*], and less mythological, although its language is more heightened and it draws more heavily on Christian doctrine. That the novel should have been a product of what Robert Lowell termed the "tranquilized fifties" is remarkable, because in certain ways *Go Tell It on the Mountain* imitates its era. There is an external and formal tidiness to this book which belies a monstrous internal chaos, a chaos made up, not as in *Native Son*, primarily of action, but of ideas, feelings, spiritual messages and intuitions which hound and confuse the characters. We are shown a half-dozen people mountain climbing under the sight and power of a colossal god who straddles both testaments. We watch them strive toward that god, as God the Father, and at the same time see the god grow larger, more terrible, and further out of reach.

Baldwin's story is of fathers and sons, specifically of Gabriel and John Grimes, and there are two sides to the story. The account of Gabriel's life begins with his waiting to see whether or not a local mob of white men will burn down his house. Gabriel is "the apple of his mother's eye." He grows up wildly, earning the hatred and envy of his sister, Florence. When Florence turns twenty-six, and can take neither Gabriel nor their home any longer, she moves north, delivering the care of their God-ridden mother into Gabriel's hands. Now Gabriel is forced to reform. His mother "lay waiting . . . for his

From *Black Fiction.* © 1974 by the President and Fellows of Harvard College. Harvard University Press, 1974. Originally entitled "Lord of the Rings" and "White Outside."

surrender to the Lord." The surrender comes in a miraculously quick conversion
when Gabriel receives a sign in the form of a tree to lean on: "this was the
beginning of his life as a man." He becomes a preacher, and a year after the
death of his mother, he marries Deborah, the holy lady and pariah of the town
who, at the age of sixteen, had been dragged into the fields and raped by the
same white men who years earlier had threatened to burn down Gabriel's house.

Equipped with a resonant voice and a talent for sermons, Gabriel becomes
renowned as a preacher, yet he remains open to temptation. He meets a serving
girl, Esther, and he falls. Esther bears him a son named Royal, whom Gabriel
disowns and whose existence Gabriel denies. In fear of having his sin discovered,
he sends Esther away to die. Later, Royal gets "hisself killed in Chicago." Deborah
learns the truth, but does not reveal it, even when dying. As did Florence before him, Gabriel comes north to New York, meets and marries Elizabeth,
who already has one son, John, and who bears Gabriel another, whom once
again Gabriel calls Royal. The novel opens as this second Royal is stabbed
in a street fight. Gabriel, Elizabeth, Florence, and John go to church in order
to pray for Royal's moral improvement. That night in church Gabriel sees John
receive the Word which had remained unavailable to himself.

Everything in Gabriel's life is a contradiction. His life is hell because the
elements of each contradiction are at war inside him. His name, Gabriel Grimes,
is a contradiction of terms: the angel of filth. The name Gabriel means "man
of god," and that, too, is a contradiction, as Gabriel is not a man of God in
any sense but the professional. He can appear to be different sizes and shapes
simultaneously: at once the pettiest figure in the novel, and the one who
dominates everyone around him. He possesses both the smallest and largest
conscience, the longest and shortest memory, the highest and lowest sense of
righteousness. Opposing forces flourish in him, as they do in Florence, who
in the act of lovemaking "burned with longing and froze with rage," whose
"tears came down like burning rain." At an advanced age Gabriel is baptized
in water, and becomes preacher to the Temple of the Fire Baptized.

What he wants is redemption through repentance, because he believes
that for him redemption will mean that all the irreconcilables will be resolved.
He develops an elaborate system of holy living whereby he can impose simplistic
penalties upon himself. The penalties are imposed whenever Gabriel has sinned,
that is, behaved honestly according to his own passionate nature. Consistent
with his inconsistencies, he creates lies to confront and correct his truth. At
heart, he is like Gatsby without stamina, wishing to be reborn after every trans-
gression, seeking deliverance, in the sense of birth, from his own frail mind.

Yet at the same time he longs to perpetuate himself. Each son born to
him is named Royal because Gabriel wants to create a lineage of kings. In

terms of his own simpleminded mythologizing, it ought to have been glorious to have had a son named Royal by Esther, who was named for a queen, but the union was unholy, and Gabriel had to seek another heir. John can provide no lineage for Gabriel because John, who was born out of wedlock to Richard and Elizabeth, is not his natural son. The second Royal is his natural son, but the son turns upon the father, calling him a "black bastard." Bastards are denied the kingdom of heaven: "A bastard shall not enter into the congregation of the Lord; even to their tenth generation shall they not enter into the congregation of the Lord" (Deuteronomy 23:2). John is technically a bastard, yet John's salvation is the great hope of the novel.

How can John the bastard be expected to achieve heaven, and how can heaven be denied to Gabriel, the angel of the Lord? The contradictions keep accumulating. The Gabriel of the Bible is God's herald who brings great news: "Fear not, Zacharias: for thy prayer is heard; and thy wife Elisabeth shall bear thee a son, and thou shalt call his name John. And thou shalt have joy and gladness; and many shall rejoice at his birth. For he shall be great in the sight of the Lord, and shall drink neither wine nor strong drink; and he shall be filled with the Holy Ghost, even from his mother's womb. And many of the children of Israel shall he turn to the Lord their God" (Luke 1:13–16). John Grimes brings no joy or gladness to Gabriel or anyone else. He is a gloomy, sullen child, called "frog eyes" (reminiscent of a plague), at whose illegitimate birth no one rejoiced. The ghost that fills him is the terror of Gabriel, and as for turning others to the Lord, it is his own conversion which is the center of his and everyone else's attention.

To Zacharias and Elisabeth was born John, who became John the Baptist:

> I indeed baptize you with water unto repentance: but he that cometh after me is mightier than I, whose shoes I am not worthy to bear: he shall baptize you with the Holy Ghost, and with fire. Whose fan is in his hand, and he will thoroughly purge his floor, and gather his wheat into the garner; but he will burn up the chaff with unquenchable fire. Then cometh Jesus from Galilee to Jordan unto John, to be baptized of him. But John forbade him, saying, I have no need to be baptized of thee, and comest thou to me? And Jesus answering said unto him, Suffer it to be so now: for thus it becometh us to fulfill all righteousness. And Jesus, when he was baptized, went up straightway out of the water: and, lo, the heavens were opened unto him, and he saw the Spirit of God descending like a dove, and lighting upon him.
>
> (Matt. 3: 11–17)

John the Baptist was the answer to a prayer against barrenness, but the presence of John Grimes only serves to remind Gabriel of his own spiritual barrenness. Gabriel despises John both because John is a bastard and therefore unclean, and because John's existence, like a bad sign, persistently reminds Gabriel of his own bastard, the one he made and let die. As a young man, Gabriel was dragged kicking and shouting into the holy waters, where he sputtered and was blessed in the name of John, whose namesake he is obliged, by marriage, to love. No heavens opened up to Gabriel on that day, and no Spirit of God descended: "and though at first they thought that it was the power of the Lord that worked in him, they realized as he rose, still kicking, and with his eyes tightly shut, that it was only fury, and too much water in his nose." The water scorched Gabriel, and in turn, he brings a furious, evangelical fire to John, but John feels "no warmth for him from this fire."

Gabriel is supposed to be the emissary from heaven, and yet, like Bigger, he only suffers damnation. He too, was part of the "great migration" north, emigrating from one hell into another for purposes of salvation. He calls Broadway hell because the Great White Way is not the narrow way. But Gabriel is his own hell, no matter where he is located. Like Bigger, too, he was born to be close to fire. White men threaten to burn down his home. Esther "was associated in his mind with flame: with fiery leaves in the autumn, and the fiery sun going down in the evening over the farthest hill, and with the eternal fires of Hell." He continually has dreams of hell, and of Satan, and the hell of which he dreams is always sexual. Inevitably, he manages to substitute a real hell for his dream, creating his own special entrapment: Esther "sat down at the table, smiling, to wait for him. He tried to do everything as quickly as possible, the shuttering of windows, and locking of doors. But his fingers were stiff and slippery: his heart was in his mouth. And it came to him that he was barring every exit to this house, except the exit through the kitchen, where Esther sat." In his self-torturing imagination Esther is the she-devil, the queen of hell's kitchen, called appropriately after the biblical queen of revenge. The Book of Esther is noteworthy in the Old Testament for the fact that it contains no mention of God.

Yet God is all over Gabriel, every minute, like the baptismal waters around and through him. Gabriel is not merely climbing a mountain of deliverance; he is climbing that mountain with another mountain of guilt on his back: "this burden was heavier than the heaviest mountain and he carried it in his heart. With each step that he took his burden grew heavier, and his breath became slow and harsh, and, of a sudden, cold sweat stood out on his brow and drenched his back." Elizabeth is also climbing a mountain, in order to reach a simple, peaceful place for her family. Florence's mountain is built up of a lifetime of vengeance against her brother. John's mountain was erected for him and is meant to lead to a state of grace. Everyone is making one sort of climb or another, and at the same time everyone speaks of bringing everyone else "low."

Everybody also speaks of wanting to change, to convert, but in *Go Tell It on the Mountain* there are no changes. Elizabeth carries John, Richard's son, through the streets of Harlem. Richard, a fatherless child, had killed himself after having been falsely accused of being a thief. Now his own fatherless child survives, and Elizabeth thinks "of the boys who had gone to prison. Were they there still? Would John be one of these boys one day? These boys, now, who stood before drugstore windows, before poolrooms, on every street corner, who whistled after her, whose lean bodies fairly rang, it seemed, with idleness, and malice, and frustration." She considers the cycles, not only thinking of John's future, but implicitly of the future of other Elizabeths: Will her baby grow up to become one of those boys whistling at her now? Will he have a son, too, and then die a suicide, leaving his own Elizabeth forever to be whistled at?

Florence wants her Frank to change, to become sophisticated and cultivated—"And what do you want me to do, Florence? You want me to turn white?"—but Frank's only change is to walk out on Florence. Florence would like to be white herself, but the bleaching creams do not work. Esther will not change (convert) for Gabriel; instead she converts Gabriel, not on the threshing floor but the kitchen floor, back to what he really is. Gabriel's whole being is consumed with the idea of change, but Gabriel will never be different from what he is despite all the ghosts and demons he conjures up to placate his ignorance: "You can't change nothing, Gabriel," says Florence, "You ought to know that by now." Nor will God change to suit Gabriel or anyone. To the fatherless people of the novel—and everyone here is fatherless—God is the everlasting father whose will is steadfast and permanent.

Everybody wants to change, because everybody wants to be saved, and salvation here is connected with change. There is supposed to be salvation and safety in the church. Deborah, who was a nurse and prophetess in the Bible, plays the same roles in the novel, in which roles lie both her safety and salvation. Salvation means a kind of deliverance toward the light. John, Gabriel, Elizabeth, Florence, and the other members of the church are all seeking the light. And yet, as Baldwin suggested in the title of one of his essays ("Carmen Jones: The Dark is Light Enough," *Notes of a Native Son*), the light can have its own kind of darkness: "The moment of salvation is a blinding light." Florence wants light as light pertains to color; thus the light she seeks is false. John's effort is to seek the light of God and of self-understanding, both of which are obscure to him. Richard does begin to find a light, but at the end Richard is found in his prison cell, like Samson in Gaza, "his eyes staring upward with no light, dead among the scarlet sheets." Gabriel wants the light of divine vision, but he is blinded by the baptismal waters, which prevent him from seeing himself clearly. In the Book of Daniel, Gabriel brings Daniel a vision, but our Gabriel is only capable of a blind rage, he who is persistently searching for visions and miraculous signs, whose inspired sermon is on Isaiah, the Eagle-Eyed.

Here, as elsewhere in black fiction, light and daylight, as aspects of whiteness, are sources of fear. Throughout much of the literature, light serves not as a benign or inspirational force, but as an instrument of entrapment and exposure, like a search lamp, pinning characters down, revealing their real or imagined guilts, and making, or threatening to make, them vulnerable to their pursuers. "You better gid a move on," Mingo warns Harriet in Langston Hughes's *Not Without Laughter*. "Daylight ain't holdin' itself back for you." In *If He Hollers Let Him Go* Bob Jones keeps his eyes "shut tight against the mornings." Deaths occur in daylight: in *Home to Harlem* Jerco's body is discovered at dawn; in *Go Tell It on the Mountain* the flogged soldier lay "exposed to the cold white air of morning."

Metaphorically, light is also occasionally linked up with a peculiar kind of ignorance. For all the claims for the value of books and learning on the part of Toomer, Hughes, Wright, and others, education in black fiction often carries with it severe penalties of loneliness and isolation. Bob Jones in *If He Hollers Let Him Go*, Emma Lou Morgan in Wallace Thurman's *The Blacker the Berry*, the narrators of Toomer's "Avey" and "Fern" (*Cane*), and of Baldwin's "Sonny's Blues," are all set apart from their people because of their gifts, schooling, and intellectual curiosity. James W. Johnson's Ex-Colored Man deliberately avoids college, and the Invisible Man's disintegration begins at his valedictory address. At certain points, the "enlightenment" of these characters has meant a loss of feeling for roots, a loss of self. As Wright's Big Boy ("Big Boy Leaves Home," *Uncle Tom's Children*) observes, if you're standing in the light, you cannot see into the dark.

In seeking the light, John associates the darkness of his body with the darkness of his soul. He feels an overwhelming guilt attached to both darknesses:

> And he struggled to flee—out of this darkness, out of this company—into the land of the living, so high, so far away. Fear was upon him, a more deadly fear than he had ever known, as he turned and turned in the darkness, as he moaned, and stumbled, and crawled through darkness, finding no hand, no voice, finding no door. *Who are these? Who are they?* They were the despised and rejected, the wretched and the spat upon, the earth's off-scouring; and he was in their company, and they would swallow up his soul.

There is no reason for these feelings to occur to him. The connection of guilt and darkness has assaulted his imagination by way of historical inheritance, not because of any sin which he has committed. John's only identifiable sin in the novel is masturbation. Even though he says that "the darkness of his sin was in the hardheartedness with which he resisted God's power," he eventually gives in to that power. Gabriel, on the other hand, really does possess a darkness of the soul. He is not only the prince of darkness here, but the angel and prophet of darkness as well.

Gabriel is, in the deepest sense of the phrase, a living panic. Moreover, he is an inarticulate panic who uses his fists automatically, and who never seems to be able to find the proper words for an occasion except when preaching. In the pulpits he has all the words, words which in fact are nothing more than words, and have no conceptual relationship to him, nor any bearings on his actions. Yet he has a great need for words, as if some magic in the words themselves can do something for him, can hold him intact. People like Richard and Esther are eternal mysteries to Gabriel because they celebrate their inarticulateness. They are always and naturally themselves, without verbal confirmations. But for Gabriel language affords protection:

> "I done told you before," he said—he had not ceased working over the moaning Roy, and was preparing new to dab the wound with iodine—"that I didn't want you coming in here and using that gutter language in front of my children."
>
> "Don't you worry about my language, brother," she said with spirit, "you better start worrying about your *life*. What these children hear ain't going to do them near as much harm as what they *see*."

John is considered to be bright because he does have words. The stone lions posted as sentinels outside the New York Public Library at 42nd Street may serve to keep John from the words and to guard the words from John, but unlike Gabriel's "lions of lust," who only serve to tear Gabriel apart, and unlike those lions to whom the prowling white men of Gabriel's town are compared, the lions of the library may also arm John with words, and give him strength. In John's divine vision on the threshing floor "the lion's jaws [which threatened him] were stopped." John not only has words, but is also seeking the Word. As Sister McCandless observes, "The Word is hard." Still, if it is hard for John, it is impossible for Gabriel, who only regards the Word as a prison:

> "Yes," [Deborah] sighed, "the Word sure do tell us that pride goes before destruction."
>
> "And a haughty spirit before a fall. That's the Word."

"Yes," and she smiled again, "ain't no shelter against the Word of God, is there Reverend? You is just got to be in it, tha's all — 'cause every word is true, and the gates of Hell ain't going to be able to stand against it."

He smiled, watching her, and felt a great tenderness fill his heart. "You just *stay* in the Word, little sister."

In the beginning was the Word, and the Word was with God (John 1:1), but Gabriel is not with God, nor is the Word with him. Gabriel's fundamental contradiction is that despite the fact that he is a man of God, he can never be with God, or achieve that peace of mind he associates with God. When Florence walked out on his household, Gabriel was forced to become another man who was a stranger to himself. He lived that stranger's life except for one weak moment when his life was not sterile or split in two. At that moment he became a creator. Only, he created a bastard whom he was not free to love, and who in turn was not free. It is that same bastardy which is Gabriel's as well as Roy's, the bastardy of color which Gabriel shares with John, Richard, Elisha, Elizabeth, Florence, and Frank — "'You black bastards,' [Richard's false accuser] said, looking at him, 'You're all the same.'" Heaven is not open to bastards; black people have no lineage; heaven is not open to black people. If the syllogism is to be believed, then to be a black man of God is a contradiction in itself. Gabriel is father (pastor) to a bastard people who by birth are deprived of the kingdom of heaven of which he, Gabriel, is supposed to be chief angel. Standing beside that miraculous tree, Gabriel received the wrong sign; he thought he was headed for heaven, and he would up in hell, which was a deeper hell for that discovery.

As for John, his hell is attached to Gabriel's, but it has its own peculiar characteristics as well. Like everyone else in this novel, John is searching for a father — not the miracle worker whom Gabriel seeks, but a man. The man who has been provided for him is not a father, not in the sense of being a model or example, yet in a curious way the relationship of Gabriel to John is that of guide to follower. It is evidently the same relationship which Baldwin shared with his own father, one whose familial grounding was not in love or admiration, but in a cyclical conception of history:

> The day of my father's funeral had also been my nineteenth birthday. As we drove him to the graveyard, the spoils of injustice, anarchy, discontent, and hatred were all around us [the aftermath of a Harlem race riot in the summer of 1943]. It seemed to me that God himself had devised, to mark my father's end, the most sustained and brutally

dissonant of codas. And it seemed to me, too, that the violence which rose all about us as my father left the world had been devised as a corrective for the pride of his eldest son. I had declined to believe in that apocalypse which had been central to my father's vision; very well, life seemed to be saying, here is something that will certainly pass for an apocalypse until the real thing comes along. I had inclined to be contemptuous of my father for the conditions of his life, for the conditions of our lives. When his life had ended I began to wonder about that life and also, in a new way, to be apprehensive about my own.

(Notes of a Native Son)

There is a fine story by Jerome Weidman, "My Father Sits in the Dark," which describes the infinite distance between sons and fathers. It is about the silences they share, in which silences lie all the trusts, hopes, promises, and recriminations which a creator and his creature forever attempt to conceal from, or are unable to communicate to, each other. Weidman's story hinges on the son's exulting in the fact that, after persistent badgering, he has at last discovered why his father sits alone in the dark kitchen at night; but the truth the reader knows is that the son does not really understand why his father sits in the dark at all, nor will he ever do so. Gabriel sits in the dark of his guilt for the kitchen-floor sin, the dark of his ignorance, the dark of the shadow of his vengeful God, of his future damnation, of his aloneness, of his lovelessness, and of his people. But John has darknesses of his own. He was born out of darkness into darkness; his birthdays go uncelebrated. Like Bigger, he hides away in the camouflaging darkness of movie houses. Most of all, he lives in the darkness of his silent confusions.

He wonders if he is ugly:

His father had always said that his face was the face of Satan—and was there not something—in the lift of the eyebrow, in the way his rough hair formed a V on his brow—that bore witness to his father's words. In the eye there was a light that was not the light of heaven, and the mouth trembled, lustful and lewd, to drink deep of the wines of Hell. He stared at his face as though it were, as indeed it soon appeared to be, the face of a stranger, a stranger who held secrets that John could never know. And, having thought of it as the face of a stranger, he tried to look at it as a stranger might, and tried to discover what other people saw. But he saw only details: two great eyes, and a broad, low forehead, and the triangle of his nose, and his enormous mouth, and the barely perceptible cleft in his chin, which was, his father said, the mark of the devil's little finger.

Ugliness, he has learned, is to be associated with damnation, but what standards can one use to determine whether things are ugly or not? Clean things are reputed to be beautiful. He, John, is called after John the Baptist, who washed sins away. But he, called Grimes, is black himself, and as someone who is assigned to clean things, he fails: "for each dustpan he so laboriously filled at the doorsill demons added to the rug twenty more; he saw in the expanse behind him the dust that he had raised settling again into the carpet; and he gritted his teeth, already on edge because of the dust that filled his mouth, and nearly wept to think that so much labor brought so little reward." His name is dirt; his house is eternally unclean, and that uncleanliness is couched in blasphemies:

> Dirt was in every corner, angle, crevice of the monstrous stove, and lived behind it in delirious communion with the corrupted wall. Dirt was in the baseboard that John scrubbed every Saturday, and roughened the cupboard shelves that held the cracked and gleaming dishes. Under this dark weight the walls leaned, under it the ceiling, with a great crack like lightning in its center, sagged. The windows gleamed like beaten gold or silver, but now John saw, in the yellow light, how fine dust veiled their doubtful glory. Dirt crawled in the gray mop hung out of the windows to dry. John thought with shame and horror, yet in angry hardness of heart: *He who is filthy, let him be filthy still*.

John may be called ugly because of his "frog eyes" and oversized mouth, but, he wonders, is not everything that is black ugly? To what real beauty can John aspire except a change of skin? And since that particular conversion is not available to him, does it make any important difference to his life that his features are irregular or unpleasing to the eye? To be black is seemingly to be unlovely enough. The policemen who arrest Richard deride Elizabeth's love for Richard, because the couple is black, and love is beautiful.

John is not beautiful, and no one loves him. Not Roy, who is too fiercely intent on survival to love, nor Elizabeth, who is too fearful to love, nor Florence, whose consuming passion is the opposite of love, and certainly not Gabriel, whose God torments him. There is a single moment in *Go Tell It on the Mountain* when a kind of love flickers—the incident of John's bumping into an old man in Central Park ("the old man smiled. John smiled back")—but that moment is over in a flash, and until the end of the novel, when John discovers the beginnings of brotherly love in Elisha, there is no other occurrence filled with as much pure affection. Among the others in the story, only Elizabeth and Richard truly love each other. Elisha and Ella Mae, two young people of the Temple, make a stab at love, but their love is quashed by the elders of the church because it threatens to be sexual.

One of John's most perplexing mysteries is what sex has to do with love. Everything that he learns about sex, he gets second hand. He overhears tales about his mother's father's "house." He listens to Elisha protest too much after having been shamed before the congregation for "walking disorderly" with Ella Mae, and wonders what walking disorderly means. He hears Roy, who "knew much more about such things," boast about his sexual prowess. He reads words he cannot understand scribbled on walls. With Roy he watches a couple "do it standing up" in an abandoned basement. And he hears his mother and father, too, rising and falling in bed in the room behind his.

Rising and falling are Christian terms, as well. Is there some connection between the sexual act and the acts of devotion, or are the two antithetical, as Gabriel insists? John falls upon the threshing floor. The question of the novel is, will he rise? He has a long distance to go. Until his moment of decision to accept the Word he had been living in a hell from which he could only escape temporarily by buying a ticket to a movie house, which like Florence's train ticket that carried her north, became a passport to him. Otherwise, he could only move laterally from one area of hell to another: the hell of his home, of his people, and of his father's God. Looking back on all three before his rise, he witnesses in revulsion the degradation of other would-be converts like himself, who groped to reach, not the Jordan, but the Styx:

> Then John saw the river, and the multitude was there. And now they had undergone a change; their robes were ragged, and stained with the road they had traveled, and stained with unholy blood; the robes of some barely covered their nakedness; and some indeed were naked. And some stumbled on the smooth stones at the river's edge, for they were blind; and some crawled with a terrible wailing, for they were lame; some did not cease to pluck at their flesh, which was rotten with running sores. All struggled to get to the river, in a dreadful hardness of heart: the strong struck down the weak, the ragged spat on the naked, the naked cursed the blind, the blind crawled over the lame.

His other hell consists of his own multiple lonelinesses: the loneliness of the unloved, of the thinker who is set apart from the rest of his kind by the fact that he lives mainly in his own head, of the user of words, of the good boy whose goodness is measured by the fact that he does nothing that is not good; the loneliness of the bastard-outcast.

> I want to go through, Lord
> I want to go through.
> Take me through, Lord,
> Take me through.

Will John be able to rise out of all this mire and confusion into a new birth and deliverance?

According to Deuteronomy, the answer is no. The bastard cannot be saved despite the fact that this bastard is named for the answer to a prayer. Bastards are misfits. Yet John knows that Jesus saves. Richard calls Jesus a bastard. Jesus was a misfit. Richard was a misfit; like Jesus he was grouped with two thieves and died innocent. Esther was also a misfit because of her free spirit. And John is a misfit. If he is to be classed with Jesus does it mean that he will also rise to glory? Or is it that to be a black misfit is to be a different order of outcast altogether, to be the misfit supreme, in a class by oneself? Emerson said, "Whoso would be a man must be a nonconformist." Richard, Esther, and John are nonconformists from birth, yet their nonconformity, instead of giving them pride, has in fact kept them low.

If John's lack of conformity has not made him a man, then it seems only reasonable that his manhood lies in toeing the mark. What John is doing, therefore, on that threshing floor is waiting to conform: to conform both to the expectations of everyone around him, black and white, and to that cyclical pattern which has kept all the characters in the novel from getting anywhere, while at the same time providing the illusion of mobility. John is getting nowhere on that threshing floor. No more than Elizabeth gets anywhere by repeatedly bearing children (she is pregnant again at the time of this story), the perpetually newborn. Gabriel impregnates Elizabeth as if each conception were an act of absolution, but with every new life which enters the Grimes household (read Harlem, the nation), nothing is altered exept space. It is significant that the bulk of the novel is taken up by three prayers which remain unanswered and affect nothing.

On the threshing floor John falls, then he rises. He rises to the accompaniment of a mystical voice which in the guise of encouragement carries an awful threat: "you got everything your daddy got." If the voice is telling the truth, and John's future is destined to become his father's past and present, then John has risen to a fall which every ensuing rise will make more steep. The spiritual "Go Tell It on the Mountain" says:

> When I was a seeker
> I sought both night and day
> I asked the Lord to help me,
> And he showed me the way.
> He made me a watchman
> Upon a city wall
> And if I am a christian
> I am the least of all.

The voice which John hears tells him to rise as if on a pilgrimage, but this voice is not the one heard by Boethius, Dante, Chaucer, or Keats in the second *Hyperion*. It is a malicious voice which advertises humility as a virtue when it means humiliation.

In the beginning John had words, but at the end, at his rise, he has run out of words: "Here there was no speech or language." Elisha, also wordless at this juncture, prophesies in tongues. What he forecasts is John's salvation, but John himself cannot find the words for that event, not his own words. He calls upon Gabriel's words instead:

> John struggled to speak the authoritative, the living word that would conquer the great division between his father and himself. But it did not come, the living word; in the silence something died in John, and something came alive. It came to him that he must testify: his tongue only could bear witness to the wonders he had seen. And he remembered, suddenly, the text of a sermon he had once heard his father preach. And he opened his mouth, feeling, as he watched his father, the darkness roar behind him, and the very earth beneath him seem to shake; yet he gave to his father their common testimony. "I'm saved," he said, "and I know I'm saved." And then, as his father did not speak, he repeated his father's text: "My witness is in Heaven and my record is on high."

The living word did not come, but his father's words came, and those words were dead. He felt something come alive in him which was death, and he felt something die in him which may have been life. Now, like his father before him, he begins to call upon signs and omens. But as he walks out of the church that morning, the skulking alley cat and gray bird he sees and the bell and siren of the ambulance he hears are signs, too, signs not of divine intervention or of a glorious multitude in unity, but of a chaotic castaway universe which is his to inherit.

Does John break the pattern laid out before him or does he fit it? Love, too, is something for which John "found no words," and in Elisha he does begin to discover the capacity for love. Baldwin found that capacity at his father's funeral:

> "But as for me and my house," my father had said, "we will serve the Lord." I wondered, as we drove him to his resting place, what this line had meant for him. I had heard him preach it many times. I had preached it once myself, proudly giving it an interpretation different from my father's. Now the whole thing came back to me, as though my father and I were on our way to Sunday school and I were memorizing the golden text: *And if it seem evil unto you to serve the Lord, choose you this day whom you will serve; whether the gods which your fathers served that were on the other side of the flood, or the gods of the Amorites, in whose land ye dwell: but as for me and my house, we will serve the Lord.* I suspected in these familiar lines a meaning which had never been there for me before. All of my father's texts and songs, which I had decided were meaningless, were arranged before me at his death like empty bottles, waiting to hold the meaning which life would give them for me. This was his legacy: nothing is ever escaped. That bleakly memorable morning I hated the unbelievable streets and the Negroes and whites who had, equally, made them that way. But I knew that it was folly, as my father would have said, this bitterness was folly. It was necessary to hold on to things that mattered. The dead man mattered, the new life mattered; blackness and whiteness did not matter; to believe that they did was to acquiesce to one's own destruction. Hatred, which could destroy so much, never failed to destroy the man who hated and this was an immutable law.
>
> (*Notes of a Native Son*)

In a sense John does break the pattern because in whatever love he achieves, he possesses something which ought to be too powerful for history. In a deeper sense, however, he fits the pattern by breaking it. Richard and Esther were destroyed by love, not hate. In a sane world, if hate destroyed the man who hated, love would restore the man who loved, and things would balance. But in a situation where everything is backward and upside down, hate destroys the hater, and love destroys the lover just as surely. This is the end, a dead one, which Baldwin foresees for John, which end was in the beginning. . . .

Another Country

One comes a long way from the Temple of the Fire Baptized to *Another*

Country. Geographically, about five miles, from Harlem to Greenwich Village; spiritually, the distance from a depiction of the Saints to sinners of all varieties, and from a concentration on the straight and narrow to a survey of the wide open spaces of moral behavior. The context is modernity and the fact is sex. John, who may be on the rise at the end of *Go Tell It on the Mountain*, has been replaced as hero by Rufus, who kills himself at the outset of *Another Country*. Baldwin has largely dropped his biblical style, although some allusions remain. The sense of organization has changed as well: from focusing on individual characters, one by one, to a wide angle view of an entire people.

The title of the novel derives from one of three sources, and possibly from all of them. In Marlowe's *Jew of Malta* one of the friars confronts Barabas with "Thou hast committed . . . ," and Barabas interrupts him, and completes the accusation, saying, "fornication? But that was in another country, and besides the wench is dead." With a slight variation T. S. Eliot uses this exchange as an epigraph to his "Portrait of a Lady," a conversation between two people whose sophistication belies the fact that they are incapable of feeling. *Another Country* reflects the sterility and lovelessness depicted in Eliot's poem, and, like *The Jew of Malta*, is a revenge tragedy. The title could also come from a folk saying, "If a pigmy stands on a giant's shoulders, he can see another country," but the question of who is the pigmy, and who the giant, in this novel remains unanswered.

The central figure of the book is Rufus Scott, a black jazz drummer whose last days are spent tormenting Leona, a white Southern girl who loves him. Rufus is a desperate and degenerate man, made both by his various humiliations in the company of whites. He loves Leona, but has been reduced to a condition now where he can only hurt her. When he makes love to her, he deliberately turns the act into rape, as if to play out a classic fantasy. Eventually, Leona goes mad, and partly out of remorse, partly because he has reached the bottom of his degradation, Rufus leaps to his death from the George Washington Bridge. Before dying he storms like Gabriel at the baptism: "He raised his eyes to heaven. He thought, you bastard, you motherfucking bastard. Ain't I your baby, too?"

At Rufus's death, other characters take over: Vivaldo, the "Irish wop" from Brooklyn, Rufus's closest white friend, who wants to become a writer; Cass Silenski, a New England girl married to another writer, Richard, Vivaldo's former teacher; Eric Jones, an actor recently returned from France; and Ida Scott, Rufus's kid sister, a rising blues singer who seeks revenge against the white world for her brother's suicide. Ida moves in with Vivaldo, yet seeks to destroy him for letting her brother die. The implication throughout the novel is that all of Rufus's white friends, by sins of omission, allowed him to die.

Only Eric, the homosexual, is said to have brought love to Rufus which

Rufus reciprocated; and when Eric and Rufus parted, Rufus was left destitute. Later in the story Eric is also said to bring love to Cass, who is drawn to him out of disgust with her marriage and Richard's vulgarity and shallowness. Eric is meant to symbolize a source of pure love for both sexes. He brings love to Vivaldo as well. In France, Eric finds his own love with Yves, a Paris street boy. The novel ends with Yves arriving in America at the New York airport, greeted by Eric, supposedly bringing with him a sense of sexual liberation which will herald personal and racial freedom for everyone involved.

Another Country is designed as a modern Inferno. Lovers throw themselves at each other in lust and violence. Rufus torments Leona, and Leona, merely by being white, torments him. Ida cheats on Vivaldo, and breaks his heart. Richard and Cass despise each other because of the falsity of their life, particularly of their artistic life. Ellis, the television executive who is going to launch Ida's career, treats Ida like a whore. Everyone betrays everyone else. Cass has an affair with Eric; Eric with Vivaldo; Vivaldo with Ida; Ida with Ellis. In the character of Ellis is material gluttony. Sexual gluttony is ubiquitous. There is rape, in the rape of Leona. There is perversion and hysteria: Richard slams Cass in the head, and screams at her, "Did [Eric] make love to you better than I? Is that it? And did he fuck you in the ass, did he make you suck his cock? Answer me, you bitch, you slut, you cunt!" There is even an implicit murder. At Rufus's funeral people glare at Vivaldo as if he had done the killing.

Baldwin sees the white characters as the prime, though not the sole, movers in all this evil. It is the white characters who have become unable or unwilling to probe the "dark side" of their human nature, the side which contains one's basic animalism and humanity as well, and which, if explored, might release these people from their self-made confinement. This confinement has made the whites brutal and rootless, whereas the black characters have been brutalized only by the whites, not by themselves, and so are morally cleaner. The black characters also suffer, but they understand the source of their suffering because they *are* the "dark side" of experience. The idea, put simply, is that blacks and whites must go to or create another country, in order to revamp or revitalize the one they have. Here is the deliberately arranged international cast: a Pole (Richard), a WASP (Cass), two blacks, an Irish-Italian, and a Frenchman. With them a new melting pot must be made, one characterized by personal and national freedom.

The structure of the novel consists of book 1, which focuses on the low and hopeless life (Rufus), and books 2 and 3, which represent a redemptive movement (Eric). Redemption is to be achieved by freedom on all fronts, especially sexual freedom. Homosexuality, in the person of Eric, becomes the main liberating force of the story. Blackness, too, is an expression of freedom,

so blackness and homosexuality become thematically related. Book 2 begins
with a picture of Eric in Eden: "Eric sat naked in his rented garden. Flies buzzed
and boomed in the brilliant heat, and a yellow bee circled his head." Eric is
the new Adam, waiting for the arrival of Yves (Eve). Homosexuality, considered
a vice, becomes a virtue, thus making a heaven of hell.

How stable a heaven homosexuality creates is problematical, however.
The pervasive condition of *Another Country* is chaos, a chaos in which various
freedoms oppose various restraints in search of a new order. Eric, who "had
discovered, inevitably, the truth about many men, who then wished to drive
Eric and the truth together out of the world," is said to represent the new
order, while everyone else floats in a vacuum of what Robert Lowell called
"lost connections." In *Go Tell It on the Mountain* Baldwin's characters were islands inhabiting the island of Harlem. Here, there is the other island of
Manhattan, and again the people are islands to each other. It is said that Rufus
"made some very bad connections," and it is fitting that he uses a bridge to
end his life.

Ida's singing is also described as if it were an island, powerful and mysterious. Cass and Richard intentionally drift apart from each other. Richard will
not speak Polish, wishing to deny and be free of his national identification.
Everyone seeks to be a stranger, although at Rufus's funeral the mourners sing,
"I'm a stranger, don't drive me away," and Rufus's mother tells Vivaldo to visit
them often, "Don't you be a stranger." The goodbyes people share in the novel
are always prolonged tediously, like the stringing out of a lifeline. Homosexuality, too, creates a state of isolation in the unproductive act. People
continuously speak of being exiled, and when Cass waves goodbye to Vivaldo
it's "like waving goodbye to the land."

The people are islands, and the islands are at war. Richard and Vivaldo
are in a talent war, each striving to out-write the other. Rufus and Leona have
inherited a state of war, which they continue. Cass and Richard are in a
permanent battle; Ida fights Ellis, Vivaldo fights Ida, and so on. Even the young
people are at war. The Silenski children are beaten in a gang fight with black
children. Baldwin uses metaphors of war to describe the various relationships:
battlefields, truces, retreats, treasons, triumphs, betrayals, wounds, loyalty,
banishment, minefields. The epigraph of book 2 – "Why don't you take me
in your arms and carry me out of this lonely place" – is from Conrad's *Victory*.
Vivaldo feels threatened among Ida's musician friends: "He had no function,
they did: they pulled rank on him, they closed ranks against him." When Ida
makes love to Vivaldo, hers is the "technique of pacification."

Because they exist in a state of war, all of the characters are wary and
afraid. Leona is terrorized by Rufus, Rufus is terrorized by everyone, and

everybody hides from everybody else out of fear of exposure. At the beginning of the story Rufus plays the drums accompanying a saxophone, and hears the repeated refrain, "Do you love me? Do you love me? Do you love me?" On route to Rufus's funeral, the radio in Cass's taxi plays, "Love me." Vivaldo prays, "Oh God, make [Ida] love me." Yet, with all the talk of love, Rufus, wracked with hate and self-hate, is beyond connections. Leona, punchy from a brutal early marriage, cannot survive with Rufus, and ends up alone in madness. Richard is isolated in his literary pretensions, and despite his liberal protestations, is filled with race hatred. Cass, who married beneath her, cannot be honest with her husband. Vivaldo, who progressed from a Brooklyn street gang to the Village, has no place of his own, no ties. Ellis, the agent and impresario, has the loneliness of the parasite. Ida, bent on success and revenge, has objectives which demand secrecy and allow no trust in anyone.

The isolation of the characters from one another is complemented by their isolation as artists. Six of the major characters in *Another Country* are artists themselves, and all of the others live off of or with artists. Most of these artists are inept (the characters whom Vivaldo creates in his fiction do not "trust" him), but good or bad, being an artist is itself an insular condition. Except for Rufus, who occasionally is able to lose himself in his drumming, and Ida, who also occasionally can transport herself by singing, the rest of the characters function as spies, predators; actors, painters, and writers taking notes on experience, and gathering material second hand. In *Notes of a Native Son* Baldwin said, "The only real concern of the artist [is] to recreate out of the disorder of life that order which is art." Instead of making order out of chaos, these artists accomplish the reverse.

Out of the chaos they create emerge Eric and Yves, who are said to bring emancipation to the new world. The notion is a curious turnabout as it relates to American thought. In his famous Phi Beta Kappa address, Emerson advised the nation no longer to court the muses of Europe, rather to shake off the degeneration of the old world in the name of fresh starts and native resources. In *Another Country* the apparent solution is to seek the European muse, thereby to free the new world of its moral imprisonments. The matter, to Baldwin, is the freedom to love: "When people no longer knew that a mystery could only be approached through form, people became—what the people of this time and place had become, what he [Vivaldo] had become. They perished within their despised clay tenements in isolation, passively, or actively together, in mobs, thirsting and seeking for, and eventually reeking of blood. Of rending and tearing there can never be any end, and God save the people for whom passion becomes impersonal."

Eric, then, is supposed to bring love; yet for all the statements in his behalf, he is as alone as any of the others in the novel, and knowingly or not he has sent for Yves to share his loneliness. Eric may have "found himself"—that discovery is called his saving grace—but he has brought nothing lasting or revitalizing to those with whom he comes in contact. As Yves enters the country, he is anxious but reassured by the sight of Eric waiting for him on the airport's observation deck: "Then he was in a vaster hall, waiting for his luggage, with Eric above him, smiling down on him through glass. Then even his luggage belonged to him again, and he strode through the barriers, more high-hearted than he had ever been as a child, into that city which the people from heaven had made their home." Eric welcomes Yves into the cage, into another country which will corrupt him.

At one point Cass confronts Ida with the possibility that things can change for the better. Ida responds that the cyclical pattern of history is strong enough to preclude change, and Cass thinks, "I don't believe it. . . . If you're talking of yourself and Vivaldo—there are other countries—have you ever thought of that?" Ida scorns the idea, saying that by the time she and Vivaldo could raise the money to go, there would be nothing left of their feeling for each other. But her argument is academic. The truth is that there is no other country for Ida, Vivaldo, or any of these characters. It is America itself, says Baldwin, which is another country, one other than the country it believes itself to be. If these people, black and white, seek another country still, they must look inward.

The irony of such a message applies directly to the entire history of black writing. The first black novels produced in America concerned themselves with proving that black people were as good as the whites, as honorable, intelligent, and decent. The characters in the early novels were either as white in actual color as their authors could make them, or, as the line in "Black and Blue" goes, "white inside"; but the point was always the same, that day by day black people were becoming increasingly white because to become white was a sign of general improvement. By the 1920s, however, a writer like Walter White was leading his octoroon (*Flight*) back to her ghetto and away from the white world in which she had become uncomfortably assimilated. By 1940 Bigger Thomas and Lustre Johnson (of Ann Petry's *The Street*) were taking on the white world with murder in their hearts. And by 1960, Kelley and Baldwin, having come full circle with a twist, are again saying that their heroes and heroines are surviving because they have become just as good as the whites with whom they deal, just as self-seeking, treacherous, and dishonorable.

Seventy years intervene between Dunbar and Kelley, yet if there is any perceivable difference in the treatments of white America in their work, or in that of Petry and Baldwin, it is merely a difference of degree. In all four books art arises as an important force. Freddie Brent and Johnnie Roane wish to become artists because they believe they can remake the world. Mitchell Pierce, a writer for an ad agency, does not hold that belief. His "art" is commercial, as is the art of the characters in *Another Country*. As Baldwin says, art is supposed to shape life, but in these books the life has diminished the art within it, and has forced an accommodation which has made art unable to shape anything. The association of blackness with art is an association with a form of freedom, so the suppression of art becomes one more form of confinement. Without art, the world which is white outside is not only lifeless and self-destructive; it is, in terms of art itself, out of control.

MARION BERGHAHN

Images of Africa
in the Writings of James Baldwin

The first thing to remember here is that Baldwin developed his concept of
the Black American largely in reaction to Wright, his "spiritual father." It has
been mentioned above that he was very critical of Wright's idea of seeing the
Afro-American predicament purely in terms of dehumanisation. This he rejected,
by implication. It was tantamount to pushing the Afro-Americans into a total
void and, unlike Wright, Baldwin finds this position intolerable. Basically all
human beings, he writes, yearn to be accepted by the society in which they
live. However, Baldwin is not an assimilationist. Total assimilation, he argues,
would be based on the assumption "that the black man, to become truly human
and acceptable, must first become like us." But this would amount to an
"obliteration of his own personality, the distortion and debasement of his own
experience." It implied a "surrendering to those forces which reduce the person
to anonymity." It was only on his specific existence as a black in the United
States that the black man's true self and his human dignity were based. He
would remain an outcast, a "non-being," as long as he did not identify with
his existence as an Afro-American and with his past. He would have to integrate
his life as a member of American society into this self-image of his. In other
words, what Baldwin tries to do is to generalise the very personal evolution
of his own consciousness.

It reminds one of John's subjection to Noah's Curse when Baldwin explains:

> We cannot escape our origins, however hard we try, those origins
> which contain the key — could we but find it — to all that we later

From *Images of Africa in Black American Literature.* © 1977 by Marion Berghahn. Rowman
and Littlefield, 1977. Originally entitled "The Transitional Phase — Time of Scepticism."

become. . . . It is a sentimental error, therefore, to believe that the
past is dead; it means nothing to say that it is all forgotten, that
the Negro himself has forgotten it. . . . The man does not remember
the hand that struck him, the darkness that frightened him, as a
child; nevertheless, the hand and the darkness remain with him.

However, it is not just a matter of making sense of the present by including
the historical aspect. Conversely, the task is also to come to terms with the
Afro-American past. For "the past will remain horrible for exactly as long as
we refuse to assess it honestly." Baldwin can thus be placed in a tradition which
started at the end of the nineteenth century and which flourished during the
Harlem Renaissance, of identifying with one's past rather than repressing it
in shame. But Baldwin carries this argument further than previous writers.
He urges Afro-Americans to refrain from protest and to subscribe to the black
experience and its consequences. The Negro, he says, should make his peace
with "darkness" and with the "nigger in himself." And he should do so without
allowing himself, like Bigger, to be overwhelmed and dehumanised by it.
Otherwise hatred and self-hatred would destroy him — just as Bigger was
destroyed by it.

Baldwin realises that adopting this position involves taking over the biblical
notion of the blacks being the symbol of "the evil, the sin and suffering." Afro-
Americans would have to "accept the status which myth, if nothing else, gives
[them] in the West before [they] can hope to change the myth." Death, violence
and hate are the crosses which Afro-Americans have to bear, not merely for
the sake of their own humanity, but also, and above all, to save white America.
In fact, Baldwin interprets America's problems as deriving from the refusal of
the whites to recognise the "dark" and "subterranean" spheres of life. They had
created a world of illusions around them and refused to abandon them in favour
of a more "realistic" view of life. The role of the blacks in the United States
is therefore to liberate the whites from their "ignorance" and "innocence." They
were messengers from "that terrifying darkness from which we come," where
they had experienced suffering, violence and hatred. It was their duty to testify
to the existence of this world which the whites ignored. They were supposed
to contribute this knowledge to the "American experience" in order to generate
a genuine sense of reality. In other words, the blacks, purified by their suffering,
are expected to provide a kind of "moral rearmament" of white America. In
postulating this, Baldwin starts from the assumption that the whites did not
know what they were doing when supporting racism. Through love and
compassion, Afro-Americans should therefore make them aware of reality and
carry some light into their "spiritual darkness": "If it is true, and I believe it

is, that all men are brothers, then we have the duty to try to understand this wretched man; and while we probably cannot hope to liberate him, begin working toward the liberation of his children."

This appeal to "love thine enemies" and to refrain from rebellion, reflects quite distinctly those Christian elements in Baldwin's thinking which his upbringing had instilled in him. But it is also indicative of his belief in something like an "*Ur*-love" between whites and blacks which the Fall of Man—in this case his racial hatred—had destroyed. The white father chased his black son (and thereby ultimately himself) from paradise—an argument which again is partly reminiscent of Noah's curse. But man must find his way back to this "*Ur*-love." Love—as Baldwin tries to show in his novels with their frequently racially mixed couples—is the only cure against the evils of this world.

What, in view of the black "group reality" of Baldwin's novels, raises considerable problems is that love and reconciliation are to be achieved through the suffering of the Afro-Americans who are supposed to accept their own "darkness." His own criticism of Wright that he disregarded the humanity of blacks could also be levelled against Baldwin. Accepting one's "black" existence is, after all, most unlikely to have a humanising effect. On the contrary, it was bound to lead to a further isolation and alienation of the Afro-Americans. In the final analysis they would be driven into hatred and self-hatred just as Wright's characters had been. They are—like Baldwin himself—totally orientated towards the white man, whom they want to "educate" and who, despite his "one-dimensionality," time and again emerges from the narrative as a more convincing and "fuller" character than his black counterparts. The life of the Afro-Americans serves more as a fill-in and hardly possesses a dimension of its own. In so far as a black "group reality" is at all depicted, it tends to be oppressive rather than "sustaining." It is more destructive of self-respect and geared to an adaptation to white norms (above all, where the repression of sexuality is concerned) than orientated towards generating a new self-confidence. *Another Country*, Baldwin's most important novel as far as his "love theory" is concerned, offers a good example. In this novel it is Eric, a white man, who appears as the most humane, most intuitive character, as the person who is most capable of genuine love. Rufus, the Afro-American, on the other hand, destroys the life of his girlfriend as well as his own because he is so depressed by his inability to overcome his feelings of hatred and to love her.

Another paradox in Baldwin's thinking, but again characteristic of his approach, is how he associates the relatively intact self-confidence of some of his black characters with Africa and how he turns more and more towards Black Nationalism. One reason for this may be that his rejection of hatred and his exhortation to show compassion and even love for the whites might meet with the disapproval of militant blacks "whom he both fears and respects." And since "he senses betrayal in his own attitudes he fears writing what may be interpreted as a betrayal of his own race." By blowing the nationalist trumpet, he tries to link up with separatism at a time when the intellectual and political climate in the United States underwent a marked shift away from earlier plans of integration and racial reconciliation. This conclusion emerges most clearly from a later novel, which will be analysed in greater detail in a moment. However, it must be added that a genuine interest in Africa and an appetite for "revelations of superiority" can be traced back to Baldwin's "pre-nationalist" phase. Even *Go Tell It on the Mountain* contains a reference to this when Richard—John's real and Baldwin's "ideal" father—visits the Metropolitan Museum of Art with his wife Elizabeth. But whereas his wife is not really attracted by the African department, Richard is fascinated:

> She did not know why he so adored things that were so long dead; what sustenance they gave him, what secrets he hoped to wrest from them. But she understood, at least, that they *did* give him a kind of bitter nourishment, and that the secrets they held for him were a matter of his life and death. It frightened her because she felt that he was reaching for the moon and that he would, therefore, be dashed down against the rocks.

In fact, Elizabeth's premonitions were to come true. Richard's self-confidence, bolstered by his acquaintance with Africa, gives him a new sense of human dignity. His pride is awakened in him. He is driven into rebellion against his predicament as a black. Unlike John he does not find a sense of purpose in suffering. Ultimately the tension between his will to assert himself and the frustration which he experiences becomes so intolerable that he commits suicide.

In *Another Country* it is "black, filthy foolish" Rufus who finds a life of humiliation in white society unbearable when he comes to realise that God is "white" and that life "belongs" to the whites. To Rufus, by contrast, "belongs only the black, cold water. The water of life . . . has become a dark river of death for Rufus and his race." It is "race-conscious" Ida, Rufus's sister, who proves to be stronger and thus survives; for Ida is endowed with a "profound" and "powerful" self-confidence. To give an impression of her personality Baldwin resorts to a nationalist rhetoric which he seems to have borrowed from the Harlem Movement. Ida, at any rate, was "very, very dark, she was beautiful." Baldwin stresses repeatedly that her beauty stems from her African origin:

> Ages and ages ago, Ida had not been merely the descendant of slaves. Watching her dark face in the sunlight, softened and shadowed by

the glorious shawl, it could be seen that she had once been a
monarch. Then he looked out of the window, at the air shaft, and
thought of the whores of Seventh Avenue. He thought of the white
policemen and the money they had made on black flesh, the money
the whole world made.

An interest in Africa as a potential source of a positive self-image which,
accompanied by a reluctant protest against the hard, white God, had been
more overt in *Go Tell It on the Mountain*, becomes even more noticeable in
Baldwin's writings from about 1959 onwards. Thus he wrote in a report on
the Pan-African Cultural Congress at Paris, published in 1960, that Afro-
Americans and Africans are joined together by the need "to remake the world
in their own image, to impose this image on the world, and no longer be
controlled by the vision of the world, and of themselves, held by other people.
What, in sum, black men held in common was their ache to come into the
world as men." And only a year later he asserts that "the American Negro
can no longer, nor will ever again, be controlled by white America's image
of him."

The causes of this change are seen by Baldwin to lie above all in the growing
importance of the new postcolonial African states. He considers the rise of
Africa most important. It puts the Afro-American in the position of identifying
with Africa at last and even "to think of himself as an African [which] is a
necessary step in the creation of his morale." This is particularly true of Baldwin
himself, who now moves more in the direction of a close (positive) identification
with Africa. The emergence of independent states, he maintains, shows that
Africa is not "uncivilized." Hence Afro-Americans would no longer have to
be ashamed of that continent. The younger generation of Afro-Americans lived
in very different circumstances:

> By the time they were able to react to the world, Africa was on
> the stage of history. This could not but have an extraordinary effect
> on their own morale, for it meant that they were not merely the
> descendants of slaves in a white, Protestant, and puritan country:
> they were also related to kings and princes in an ancestral homeland,
> far away. And this has proved to be a great antidote to the poison
> of self-hatred.

But this self-confidence is not yet so strong that he does not have to resort
to overcompensation. An "ordinary" African is apparently not capable of
satisfying the demand for "civilized" behaviour. As in the above quotation (and

in *Another Country* or other works) "kings and princes" have to bear witness to this capability.

Finally, in the first half of the 1960s Baldwin decides to visit Africa. He offers the following explanation for his decision:

> I think there is a great deal I can discover about myself there. There is something beautiful about it. I want to find out. It is at the gateway of the modern world, and I could help to be a guide. . . . I might also find that part of me I had to bury when I grew up, the capacity for joy, of the sense, and something almost dead, real good-naturedness. I think they still believe in miracles there and I want to see it.

Somewhat more subdued are the words which he wrote to his publisher in 1961:

> My bones know, somehow, something of what waits for me in Africa. That is one of the reasons I have dawdled so long—I'm afraid. And, of course, I am playing it my own way, edging myself into it: it would be nice to be able to dream about Africa, but once I have been there, I will not be able to dream any more. . . . One flinches from the responsibility which we all now face, of judging black people solely as people.

This means that, deep down in his heart, Baldwin still feared that the traditional arguments about the African's lack of civilisation, which he had learned to believe in, might be confirmed and thus increase his inferiority complex. But in the course of the journey which he finally made to Africa he found that his fears were without foundation: "It was *marvellous*. Something in me recognized it. Recognized it all, I was never uneasy in myself—in view of, you know, *them*." Though exhilarated by the success of his African encounter, Baldwin does not conceive of it as a "homeland." He continues to uphold his concept of the "American-ness" of Afro-Americans and of the specific role which blacks had to fulfil *vis-à-vis* the whites. What he did feel, however, was a sense of responsibility for Africa, "because . . . whatever is going to happen in Africa, I was in one way or another involved. Or *affected* by it, certainly. But . . . I didn't feel it could happen on the basis of *colour* . . . I loved Africa. I want to go back."

There is behind these simple words the attempt to perform a difficult balancing act. On the one hand, Baldwin joins the chorus of Black Nationalists. He promotes the idea of "Black is beautiful"; he develops a keen interest in Africa and advocates the formation of a united front with Africans. The newly won independence of the African states offers, he believes, at last an opportunity of liberating the blacks from the spiritual domination of the whites. On the other hand, he argues that colour is unimportant. In fact, as before, he explicitly includes the whites in his notion of universal love. Obviously it was bound to be most difficult to avoid a collision between these two approaches to the problem. Thus one finds on one and the same page: "The value placed on the colour of the skin is always and everywhere and forever a delusion"; and "black people, though I am aware that some of us, black and white, do not know it yet, are very beautiful." Nor is it particularly logical for instance – at least not from a nationalist point of view – that it is the main task of "race-conscious" Ida to rescue the white Liberals, represented here by Vivaldo, from their "innocence."

This ambivalence which is typical of Baldwin is also the keynote of his novel, *Tell Me How Long the Train's Been Gone*. Once again this novel contains a strong autobiographical element. His rhetoric is evidently influenced by the Black Power Movement and reflects his attempt to adapt to the changing consciousness of the 1960s and to establish contact with the much-vaunted "soul" community of all blacks. But he is never quite successful. We have seen repeatedly how Afro-American writers were often strongly influenced by experiences earlier on in their life. Baldwin is yet another example. He is too deeply rooted in the ideas of the 1940s and 1950s to participate in the "revolution in black consciousness" with ease. Thus one reviewer, admittedly not particularly well-disposed towards Baldwin, certainly had a point when he wrote about *Tell Me*: "The most important thematic progression to be noted in this work is that for the first time in a Baldwin novel, black man gets black boy." Again the basic themes of this particular novel are the depressing boyhood of the main character, Leo Proudhammer, in Harlem; heterosexual as well as homosexual relations; the isolation of Proudhammer, most of whose friends are whites, from other blacks; self-hatred and group-hatred among Afro-Americans. His denial notwithstanding, there is finally even an attempt to bring the whites to their senses, i.e., to make them see their prejudices and to persuade them to recognise their past "sins."

Leo is completely orientated towards the whites. Descriptions of an organic and positive Afro-American group life are missing, and black characters in *Tell Me*, like those of *Another Country*, often lack vitality and conviction. This is what separates him not only from other writers of the 1960s towards whom he is trying to move, but also from Wright and Ellison who draw a much more vivid picture of Afro-American life than Baldwin. One possible explanation of this might be, as Eckman has pointed out, that he had more friends among whites than among Afro-Americans since early childhood. Accordingly he tends to look upon other blacks more through the eyes of a white man than through those of someone who is directly affected. Thus, probably in order to avoid giving the (white) reader an unfavourable impression of the Afro-American world, Baldwin feels obliged to explain the behaviour of blacks as follows:

> I saw, with a peculiar shock, the root of the despicable and tenacious American folk-lore concerning the happy, prancing niggers. Some of these people were moving, indeed, and the jukebox was loud; their movements followed the music which their movements had produced; but prancing scarcely fairly described their uses of their vigor. Only someone who no longer had any sense of what consti-tuted happiness could ever have confounded happiness with this rage. . . . It was my own uneasiness as we entered which afforded me my key to the domestic fantasy.

No less characteristic of his relationship with Afro-Americans and whites alike is his endeavour to weave references to black culture into his narrative. Thus Leo has little contact with Afro-Americans and it is somewhat difficult for Baldwin to integrate black culture into his plot. Accordingly, black folklore appears in places where it is really somewhat misplaced. For example, Leo goes to a party given by famous and wealthy whites at which he is the only black person. And suddenly he feels the urge to play and sing a blues to a (white) girl whom he has met at this party. To do so, he says somewhat clumsily, "helps—to—keep me in touch with myself." Then, much to the delight of his (white) audience, he begins to sing: "Blues, you're driving me crazy, what am I to do? . . . I ain't got nobody to tell my troubles to." Baldwin does not seem to be aware of the irony in this scene.

Striking passages influenced by Black Nationalism, such as this one, are added to Baldwin's traditional repertoire, evidently in an attempt to narrow the gap between himself and other blacks. Whereas Rufus—shortly before his death—quarrels with his fate as a black and levels accusations against the white world, Leo, suffering a heart attack (at the beginning of the novel), is reminded of the myth that the soul of dead Afro-Americans returns to Africa. Moreover, it is remarkable how often Baldwin uses the word "black," mainly in description of persons: "Black Christopher: because he was black in so many ways—black in color, black in pride, black in rage . . . Christopher looked like a black sun . . . , opened his big black face and clapped his big black hands." The fact that the main character of the novel calls himself an "Ethiopian" and that the father-figure is depicted as a militant nationalist and former Garveyite is also new. Certainly, James Baldwin never mentions anywhere in his earlier writings that David Baldwin held such sympathies. Just as David Baldwin maintained that he was a descendant of African kings, so Leo's father tells his children that

> he came from a race which had been flourishing at the very dawn
> of the world—a race greater and nobler than Rome or Judea,
> mightier than Egypt—he came from a race of kings, kings who had
> never been taken in battle, kings who had never been slaves. He
> spoke to us of tribes and empires, battles, victories, and monarchs
> of whom we had never heard—they were not mentioned in our
> schoolbooks.

Yet these words made little impact. The contrast between these dreams of
a glorious and proud past and the misery of the present was too stark:

> If our father was of royal blood and we were royal children, our
> father was certainly the only person in the world who knew it. . . . It
> was scarcely worthwhile being the descendant of kings if the kings
> were black and no one had ever heard of them, and especially,
> furthermore, if royal status could not fill the empty stomach.

In these circumstances Africa did not have much attraction. As before, Baldwin
is not prepared to emigrate from the United States. There has been little change
in his ambiguous position *via-à-vis* America as his "strange home."

If these lines may be taken to imply a mild criticism of the cultural
nationalism of the 1960s, Baldwin nevertheless came to show great sympathy
for a militant kind of nationalism and is even prepared to accept the need for
armed resistance against white domination. This is clearly a surprising metamorphosis in Baldwin's thinking after his earlier preference for moral appeals
over political action or even politically motivated analyses of the black
predicament. In *The Fire Next Time* he still spoke up against violence by blacks.
He was convinced of a vengeance "that cannot be prevented by any police
force or army: historical vengeance, a cosmic vengeance, based on the law that
we recognize when we say 'Whatever goes up must come down.'" Since then
Baldwin has come to believe that the younger generation of Afro-Americans
(represented by "black Christopher" in *Tell Me*) had a right to search for
alternative solutions. He even admits ashamedly that earlier generations have
been unable to effect a basic change of conditions by peaceful means. Hence
his conclusion: "I had to agree because I loved him and valued him. I had to
agree because it is criminal to counsel despair. I had to agree because it is always
possible that, if one man can be saved, a multitude can be saved. . . . Perhaps
God would join us later, when He was convinced that we were on the winning
side."

The sarcasm of the final sentence demonstrates that Baldwin's increasingly militant nationalism is accompanied by a rebellion against his Christian God. It was barely noticeable in his earlier writings, but now it is unrestrained:

> A faint breeze struck, but it did not cool my Ethiopian brow. Ethiopian hands: to what God indeed, out of this despairing place, was I to stretch these hands? . . . I had had quite enough of God— more than enough, more than enough, the horror filled my nostril, I gagged on the blood-drenched name; and yet was forced to see that this horror, precisely, accomplished His reality and undid my unbelief.

Although he does not abandon his faith in God, he is very outspoken in his criticism of Christianity as an institution and against those "goddam missionaries" who had destroyed the Africans and hence also himself. The task of today, he writes, is "to prevent these Christians from once again destroying this pagan," i.e., Christopher who embodies the "proud" and "beautiful" black—a new "New Negro," as one might also call him, who represents a world different from that in which Baldwin had grown up. The close association of this "New Negro" with "Black Christ" throws an interesting light on Baldwin's frame of reference within which his "New World" is supposed to emerge. It does not seem to be mere coincidence that the name "Christopher" appears most of the time in connection with the adjective "black."

What Baldwin's "new" values were supposed to be can be looked up in the more important writings which he has published since *Tell Me*. What immediately strikes the eye in them is that his criticism has become even more radical. It is partly directed against Christianity which he accuses of having betrayed all its ideals: "The Christian church has betrayed and dishonored and blasphemed that Saviour in whose name they have slaughtered millions and millions and millions of people." The Christian world is thus "nothing but a tissue of lies, nothing but an excuse for power, as being as removed as anything can possibly be from any sense of worship, still more, from any sense of love." But then Baldwin moves beyond Christianity and finds harsh words for Western civilisation as a whole. His position is now the exact opposite of what it was before, as can be seen from the literal repetition of certain of his key notions, except that they have been "transvalued" completely. For example, Baldwin had written in his first volume of essays that, because the blacks lacked a culture of their own, they had no choice but to adopt Western values. Now he maintains that the history of the West is

> nothing but an intolerable yoke, a stinking prison, a shrieking grave. . . . And whatever this history may have given to the sub-

jugated is of absolutely no value, since they have never been free
to reject it; they will never be able even to assess it until they are
free to take from it what they need, and to add to history the
monumental fact of their presence. The South African coal miner,
or the African digging for roots in the bush, or the Algerian mason
working in Paris, not only have no reason not to bow down before
Shakespeare, or Descartes, or Westminster Abbey, or the cathedral
at Chartres: they have, once these monuments intrude on their
attention, no honorable access to them. Their apprehension of
this history cannot fail to reveal to them that they have been robbed,
maligned, and rejected: to bow down before that history is to accept
that history's arrogant and unjust judgment.

And the West's claim to cultural superiority, he continues, is nothing but "a
mask of power." Liberating the blacks (and in this case, the African) from
economic exploitation would lead to their liberation from Western cultural
domination. "Later, of course, one may welcome [Western cultural traditions]
back, but on one's own terms, and absolutely on one's own land." In other
words, Baldwin had moved to the other extreme. But at the same time he
had left open his retreat.

Nor does he have the slightest doubt that the blacks will achieve self-
determination. White corruption and demoralisation spelt disaster for the West.
The future belongs to the blacks. In fact they had already begun "to forge a
new morality, to create the principles on which a new world will be built."
But as Margaret Mead rightly asked Baldwin: "Where do you get your conception of morality?" Apparently this question had not occurred to him before,
as can be seen from the following dialogue: "B.: 'I get my conception of morality
from – from the way I watched . . . I get it partly from . . . where indeed do
I get it?' M.: 'Where do you get it?' B.: 'That is a good question.' " At first
he refuses to believe that his conception of morality is based on the same
Christian ethic which he condemns for its "inhumanity." In the end, however,
he cannot but agree with Margaret Mead when she tells him that "the good
that we have, the good things you are insisting on – that people should love
each other and recognise each other as brothers – is a Christian idea."

Unlike many other Black Nationalists of the 1960s and 1970s, Baldwin
did *not* base the "new morality" of his black counter-world on a system of values
which is in some way derived from African norms. Basically he does no more
than call for a revival of Christian ideals, or, as he puts it a year later, "to make
the kingdom new, to make it honorable and worthy of life." His candid
criticism of the West notwithstanding, his attitude towards Africa likewise

continues to be contradictory. Thus he now proclaims those same representa-
tives of Africa who once raised his spirits to be nothing but puppets of the
former colonial powers. A politician from Dakar, he argues, is "not necessarily
a man from Senegal. He is much more likely to be a spiritual citizen of France,
in which event he cannot possibly convey the actual needs of this part of Africa,
or of Africa." To this day Africa is chained to Europe "and as long as this is
so, it is hard to speak of Africa except as a cradle and a potential." Only when
the Africans have assumed complete control of their country and their resources
"will the African personality flower or genuinely African institutions flourish
and reveal Africa as she is." In short, in Baldwin's view Africa is not yet in
a position to offer an alternative. But in contrast with his earlier ideas, he now
thinks a spiritual and hence cultural rebirth of Africa to be possible. His notion
of what is "civilised" or "uncivilised," which had worried him so much in earlier
years, has now become very much more balanced: "One realizes that what
is called civilization lives first of all in the mind, has the mind above all as
its province, and that the civilization, or its rudiments, can continue to live
long after its externals have vanished—they can never entirely vanish from
the mind."

PEARL K. BELL

Coming Home

Neither Philip Roth nor James Baldwin set out to be an "ethnic" writer, but both were forced into pigeonholes by the anger their work aroused among their own kind. The ironic difference is that while Roth was accused of relying on stereotypes that aggravated anti-Semitism, Baldwin was flayed by the Black Nationalists for disavowing the stereotypes that dominated conventional Negro fiction.

In his famous essay, "Everybody's Protest Novel," published in *Partisan Review* in 1949, when he was only twenty-four, Baldwin announced his determination to reject the pattern of protest that a Negro writer in America was expected to follow. Instead of depicting the black man as "merely a member of a Society or a Group" who has been condemned by the white oppressors to poverty and ignorance, Baldwin chose to understand him as "something resolutely indefinable, unpredictable." A novel like Richard Wright's *Native Son*, he argued, was crippled by its hatred and fear; its failure stemmed from "its rejection of life, the human being . . . in its insistence that it is his categorization alone which is real and which cannot be transcended."

In that bold refusal to be manacled to the racial shibboleths of the "protest novel," Baldwin even felt free, during his expatriate years in France, to write a novel about white homosexuals, *Giovanni's Room*, in the first person, if only to prove that he could do without the black-and-white chessboard on which black fiction played out its predictable despair. Yet *Giovanni's Room* was an act of bravura, not an interesting novel. Baldwin's true and magnificent voice could be heard in his essays and in autobiographical stories like "Notes of a

---

From *Commentary* 68, no. 6 (December 1979). © 1979 by the American Jewish Committee. Originally entitled "Roth & Baldwin: Coming Home."

Native Son," his poignant memoir of the summer of 1943, when his father died during a bloody riot in Harlem. Even after he returned to America in the early sixties, in eager response to the civil rights movement and the rise of black nationalism, he seemed, in the lamentative reflections about race of *The Fire Next Time*, to speak out of the privacy of his mind and heart rather than as the "voice of his people." Although it prophesied a terrifying apocalypse, the essay was distinguished by its lucid dignity. It was, however, the last time he would keep his distance from the anger and hatred he had warned against in his precocious attack on the protest novel.

Despite his effort to establish his black identity, the extremist blacks would not forgive Baldwin his past. Toward the end of the sixties, Eldridge Cleaver included a vicious attack on Baldwin in *Soul on Ice*, the autobiography-*cum*-manifesto he had written in prison. With righteous ferocity he raked Baldwin over the coals not only for his homosexuality but for his "total hatred of the blacks," his literary posture, his fraternization with white liberal intellectuals, his arrogant indifference to the "political, economic, and social reference" that in Cleaver's view was the glory of Richard Wright. As for Baldwin's characters, Cleaver added in his *coup de grâce*, they "seem to be fucking and sucking in a vacuum." Stalinist criticism, it appeared, had found new life in obscenity.

In the face of Cleaver's castigation and the savage—and envious—diatribes of other black nationalists, Baldwin's stubborn independence caved in. It was hard to believe that the paranoid hysteria of *No Name in the Street* (1972)—a curious requiem for Martin Luther King, Jr., in which Baldwin renounced King's credo of nonviolence and celebrated the guerrilla tactics of the Black Panthers—came from the same sensibility which, twenty years earlier, had declared that "the oppressed and the oppressor are bound together within the same society, they accept the same criteria . . . they both alike depend on the same reality." By this point he could even bring himself to praise *Soul on Ice* and justify Cleaver's assault on him as a "necessary warning."

Given Baldwin's cultivated urbanity and nonconformist temperament, there was no reason to assume that his commitment to the black cause would diminish his rhetorical brilliance or that he would no longer use his complex personal history and attitudes in his fiction. Yet in 1962 he did attempt, in *Another Country*, to forge a language that was more austere and "unpoetic" than the lapidary biblical cadences of his natural style. So great was the strain of his effort to write against the grain that he vitiated his intelligence with sentimentality and his psychological intensity with cynical violence. Neither was he able in two later novels—*Tell Me How Long the Train's Been Gone* (1968) and *If Beale Street Could Talk* (1974)—to achieve that fusion of emotion and language which once endowed his essays with incandescent power and clarity.

Now Baldwin has tried to conquer the novel again, and it is obvious that he has staked a great deal on his new book. *Just Above My Head* is the most ambitious effort Baldwin has made to portray the black communal life and culture whose absence from the protest novel he lamented long ago, when he deplored its inability to render "the relationship that Negroes bear to one another, that depth of involvement and unspoken recognition of shared experience which creates a way of life." A huge chronicle about the children of two Harlem families from the Korean war to the present, his new book will not please those of Baldwin's critics who feel that his obsession with sex squanders talent better spent in the service of his race. But although he devotes many pages to explicit accounts of both homosexual and heterosexual love to dramatize his familiar themes of love as torment and redemption, his primary concern is the black family and the children—Hall and Arthur Montana, Julia and Jimmy Miller—whose lifelong attachment is the constant of their separate destinies.

The novel opens with the sudden death of Arthur Montana in a London pub at the age of thirty-nine. A famous gospel singer, billed as "the soul emperor," he began performing in Harlem churches as a boy and quickly rose to the top. For some years before his death, his career had been in decline, perhaps because he had moved away from gospel to the secular music of the blues. But this is only suggested vaguely by Arthur's older brother and manager, Hall, who is the narrator of *Just Above My Head*. Nor are we told what physical catastrophe killed the singer, or why he had fallen into such drunken chaos toward the end of his life. Instead Hall speaks often, with the sorrowing intensity that is the hallmark of Baldwin's literary temperament, of his brother's tender sweetness, his fragility, his vulnerable innocence. But Arthur remains stubbornly unreal throughout the book, a special presence whose importance to his brother and friends and lovers we must take on faith.

The story shuttles erratically between past and present, but only when Baldwin is writing about the Montana family when the boys were young do the characters seem substantially realized—the affectionate sparring of the brothers, the holiday rituals and food and church services, the loving devotion of the hard-working parents.

In contrast to this happy family, their friends the Millers are torn apart by pride, illness, and covetous ambition. Their daughter Julia, at the age of nine, is one of the most sought-after child evangelists in New York, and since it is only in her extraordinary sermons—naïve, arrogant, and funny—that Baldwin's prose catches fire in the novel, they come to an end too soon. When Julia's mother dies, she is trapped at fourteen in a brutal incestuous relationship with her father; escaping from him she becomes a prostitute, then a successful model, and for several years the mistress of an African chieftain in Abidjan. But all of these extraordinary permutations take place offstage, and nothing in Julia's later life can begin to match the marvel of her preaching.

Many wonderful and terrible things also happen to Hall and Arthur and Julia's little brother Jimmy, yet *Just Above My Head* is a curiously static work, partly because Baldwin seems unable to define his conception of Hall Montana: whether he is an autonomous being to whom things happen or an ill-fitting mask for the intrusive author busily shifting the scenery, revising the dialogue, and commenting sententiously on every turn of the wheel. Only the scenes in Harlem, and some later episodes in the South, when Arthur travels to Birmingham and Atlanta to sing at church rallies during the early civil rights days, have the certainty of touch and the sharply observed detail that can allow the characters to breathe on their own. Too much of the time Baldwin the black advocate loads his pages with crude menace ("Some hale and hearty white people . . . are going to be butchered corpses soon—like tomorrow, but it is utterly absurd to pity them") or woolly abstraction (Julia had "the terrified intransigence which is the key to beauty") or meandering tirades against Marxists and liberals, neither of whom are part of the story.

Though the novel seems to have been conceived as a portrayal of black family life, Baldwin loses sight of his purpose so easily that it is stillborn. Ironically, when Hall and Julia finally settle down in nearby towns in Westchester, in the comfortable stability of middle age, they are neither black nor white, just middle class, and Baldwin seems undisturbed by the deracination. But everything he says about race in the book and elsewhere would contradict such indifference to the loss of authenticity. The problem, I suspect, arises from Baldwin's inability to decide exactly where he belongs in the black world today, and what role he must fill. His nervous irresolution was clear in a recent interview; at one moment the black crusader declaring the obsolescence of white America, in the next warning writers against such slogans, and affirming that literature is indispensable to the world. Caught between these claims to his intelligence, his language, and his dedication to his people, Baldwin has written a novel that drifts and flounders in the riptide of uncertainty.

C. W. E. BIGSBY

The Divided Mind of James Baldwin

Lionel Trilling once observed that there are certain individuals who contain the "yes" and "no" of their culture, whose personal ambivalences become paradigmatic. This would seem to be an apt description of a man whose first novel was published twenty-five years ago, a man whose career has described a neat and telling parabola and whose contradictions go to the heart of an issue which dominated the political and cultural life of mid-century America: James Baldwin. And it is perhaps not inappropriate to seize the occasion of this anniversary and of the publication of his new novel, *Just Above My Head*, to attempt a summation of a writer, once an articulate spokesman for black revolt, now living an expatriate existence in southern France.

To date, Baldwin has written six novels: *Go Tell It on the Mountain* (1953), *Giovanni's Room* (1956), *Another Country* (1962), *Tell Me How Long the Train's Been Gone* (1968), *If Beale Street Could Talk* (1974), *Just Above My Head* (1979); four books of essays: *The Fire Next Time* (1963), *Nobody Knows My Name* (1961), *Notes of a Native Son* (1955), *No Name in the Street* (1972); two plays: *Blues for Mr. Charlie* (1964), *Amen Corner* (1965); and one book of short stories: *Going to Meet the Man* (1965). Born in Harlem in 1924, he left in 1948 for France, driven out by despair of the racial situation. He returned in 1957 and in the heady days of the civil rights movement found himself a principal spokesman—his polemical essay, *The Fire Next Time*, appearing at a crucial moment in black/white relations. Outflanked by the events of the late sixties, he retreated again to Europe. His more recent novels have failed to spark the popular or critical interest of his earlier work.

From *Journal of American Studies* 13, no. 3 (December 1979). © 1979 by Cambridge University Press.

What follows is not offered as a detailed critical analysis of his literary work but as an account of a career and a mind instructively divided, a sensibility drawn in opposing directions.

James Baldwin spent the first part of his career compensating for his deprivation and the second part compensating for his success. He sought invisibility in racial terms by going to Paris, and ended up by becoming the most visible black writer of his generation. His career was in part generated by the rise of the civil rights movement, as white America looked for an explanation for the crisis which had apparently arrived so suddenly; and it was eventually threatened by that movement, which in time produced demands for racial and aesthetic orthodoxy which potentially left him stranded in his equivocal role as mediator and prophet, when the dominant model for black art became fierce commitment and cultural separatism. Having fled a role as writer and individual which was determined by the colour of his skin, he discovered that that colour was in fact to be the key to his art. Wishing to dispense early with the obligation to act as spokesman, he came to recognize a responsibility to articulate, if not the demands, then the feelings of those whose own frustrations and courage were otherwise expressed in mute suffering or simple action. What Baldwin has become he once travelled four thousand miles not to be.

Both the act of refusal and the ultimate acceptance are characteristic gestures of a writer who has always been drawn in two apparently mutually incompatible directions. It was not simply that his early faith in the moral responsibility of the individual and the possibility of social change was destroyed, though he has said as much: "There was a time in my life not so very long ago that I believed, hoped . . . that this country could become what it has always presented as what it wanted to become. But I'm sorry, no matter how this may sound: when Martin was murdered for me that hope ended." It is that from the very beginning the optative mood had been in battle with a sullen determinism, the present tense constantly invaded by the past. Catonian warnings in his work have alternated with expressions of sensual salvation. His has indeed always been a schizophrenic style, as he has in turn presented himself as suffering black and alienated American, social outcast and native son. It is a rhetorical style which at its best captured the cadences of hope and rebellion which characterized the early days of the civil rights movement, and which at its worst degenerated into unashamed posturing of a kind which failed to inspect with genuine moral honesty the realities which he had once exposed with such authority.

For Baldwin, the self is sometimes a series of improvizational gestures and sometimes a moral constant which has only to be exposed to become operative.

And there is at the heart of his work, beneath the level of contingent event and social determinant, an unexamined confidence in the possibility of action and the recovery of ethical purpose. Constraints are arbitrary and irrational; hatred and rage the product of a history which is real but susceptible of transcendence. Though assailed from within and without by a corrosive mythology, the individual consciousness contains resources entirely adequate to the task of distilling meaning from social chaos, while the alliance of consciousnesses provides the principal means of resisting an isolation which is part social and part metaphysical.

At the heart of his work is a Christian belief that grace is a gift of suffering and that love has the power to annihilate the primal space between the self and its perception of itself, between the individual and the group. Racial and national categories, though real and though reflecting a symbolic heritage, exist to be transcended, for he is convinced that society clings so desperately to rigid definitions – sexual and social – more from a need to project a sense of order than from a belief that such distinctions contain any real clue to the nature of human possibilities. The Negro, in fact, is in large part a fiction, a convenient hierarchical invention. As an emblem of unrepressed needs and of uninhibited sexuality, he becomes a convenient image of the dark, spontaneous and anarchic dimension of human life. His social subordination thus stands as a symbol of society's control over its own anarchic impulses. As a consequence he is offered a role whose significance is not limited to its social utility. Thus, when he resists that caricature the consequent appeals by the dominant society to "law and order" have metaphysical as well as pragmatic implications.

In Baldwin's work the self resists the peripheral role which seems its social fate, and the primary agent in this resistance is the imagination. It is an imagination with the necessary power to project alternative worlds, to conceive of a society which can escape its own myths and consciously break its own taboos. The communicative act involved in art (virtually all of his protagonists are artists of one kind or another, including musicians, actors and novelists) becomes in itself a paradigm of a desired social interaction, while the individual's imposition of order, implied by the creative act, becomes a model for a coherence which is generated by the sensibility and not imposed by social fiat. And this presumption of an imaginative control of the world necessarily implies a rejection of that religion which historically has proved a secondary means of social control. Rejection of God is a natural extension of rebellion against the power of the state.

There is a demonstrable logic of revolt. The creation of an autonomous self relies first on a rejection of the authority of the father (his personal revolt against his father recurs in his work) and then that of white society and of

God. The self emerges, in a familiar liberal way, by a slow rejection of elements extraneous to that self. Such a process frequently involves pain and Baldwin remains enough of a puritan to believe that this is a key to truth. But salvation, paradoxically, lies in a leap from belief into scepticism. Baldwin replaces the authority of social and metaphysical diktat with an authority of the sensibility. Faith gives way to a secular belief in the authenticating power of the self.

Baldwin's characters are highly self-conscious, reflecting not only upon their social situation but on the nature of their consciousness itself. The question of identity is constantly presented to them. Indeed, it is often a clue to literal survival, so that it becomes in itself a literary event. And the particular problem which confronts them is that the usual stratagems of definition now fail. History, memory and belief are at odds with the drive for self-creation and the need for personal alliances which can deny the reality of boundaries. Thus his characters tend to adopt an ambiguous stance with regard to time, appropriating to themselves the right to define process and resist versions of historical progress which threaten to subordinate them to an alien logic.

His use of the internal monologue itself implies the existence of a resistant self which is apart from and not contained by the externalities which otherwise seem to define the limits of action and character. This is the functioning imagination, the artist within, which creates even as it analyses. His are not novels which are primarily concerned with social change in the sense of a reallocation of power; what matters to him is the altered consciousness of the individual. He is interested in process, in the interplay between the experiential and the given. The stream of consciousness becomes an image for the flow of experience and responses which provide the basis for a definition of the self. And, indeed, in a sense, one can find in William James's discussion of the stream of consciousness a justification for Baldwin's attempt to have his cake and eat it; his feeling that the self is both its own creation and an existent fact which has merely to be exposed to another level of consciousness. In *The Principles of Psychology* William James says that, "if the stream as a whole is identified with the self far more than any outward thing, *a certain portion of the stream abstracted from the rest* is so identified in an altogether peculiar degree, and is felt by all men as a sort of innermost centre within the circle, of sanctuary within the citadel constituted by the subjective life as a whole." For Baldwin this is less a spiritual essence than a sense of moral certainty, an intimate reality available to the individual who learns the necessity to engage experience with a sensibility undistorted by social presumptions.

The problem which Baldwin fails to engage is precisely how that integrity of the self can be projected onto a social scale; why the withdrawal into love should be seen as an adequate model for social action since it is frequently born out of a denial of that social action. This is something which he largely leaves to his essays. Baldwin can dramatize the moment and even the process which results in that moment; but he is, for the most part, unable to sustain that moment to the point at which it becomes an enabling strategy. The impersonal power which limits individuality seems too immune to such epiphanies to grant anything but momentary release from its definitional authority.

For Norman Mailer, the world can be made over by the personality, which can counterpose its own energies to that of society and which can release a neutralizing flood of language which, in effect, reduces the physical world to the status of backdrop: the subject of the drama is the self, the social world existing only insofar as the individual is prepared to grant it a role. Personal history becomes as authentic as public history. But for Baldwin history cannot be shrugged off with such a casual gesture. His lack of social freedom, as a Negro, contrasts markedly with that of a man who can seriously run for the office of mayor of New York, and who apparently has a kind of romantic faith in the fact that social forms are plastic enough to be moulded by the sheer power of the will. As Baldwin has never tired of telling people, the black American knows otherwise. He is all too aware of the injunctions, written and unwritten, which spell out the limits of his freedom; to cross those boundaries is to risk a reaction which is real in the sense of Dr. Johnson's definition of the term. Yet in fact he himself was tempted by solutions every bit as romantic as those advanced by Mailer, and his commitment to invoking the sinister lessons of history is always balanced by a contrary faith in a grace which can dissolve such determinism.

In his attack on Baldwin, in *Advertisements for Myself*, Mailer accused him of not being able to say "Fuck you" to the reader. It was an even more naïve remark than it seemed in that it failed to recognize that sense of oppression from which Mailer was immune but which had led Baldwin to be a writer; it also failed to recognize that all of his work was in effect an attempt to discover a basis on which such a contemptuous dismissal of society could be effectuated, while longing, as LeRoi Jones and Eldridge Cleaver cruelly pointed out, for precisely that gesture of inclusion which would obviate such a response.

For Baldwin, will, crucially allied with imagination and a sensitivity to the pressure of other selves, becomes a force with the power, if not to overcome social realities, then to forge other alliances than those sanctioned by history and power. But this is not quite the confident self of the transcendentalists. In each of his books self-analysis is not only provoked by pain; it is the source of pain. Society's power is scarcely diminished. The most that the individual can hope for is to win a small psychic territory within which the harsh pragmatics of the public world no longer operate. Nor is love quite the panacea which it appears, for it, too, is infected by materialism, by the urge to power and by the demands of history and myth. And though, as suggested above, Baldwin is never clear as to whether identity is laboriously constructed out of the interplay of sensibility and event, or whether it is a resilient moral principle concealed beneath social habiliments, in neither sense is he confident of its ability to command public acquiescence. (And this, of course, is the source of the pressure which led him to social protest outside of his novels. As a public spokesman he sought to provoke changes which would allow greater space for the self which, as a novelist, he felt was the real agent of transformation.)

Like Emerson and Thoreau he felt the need to resist those conventions and beliefs which passed for an adequate description of the real, in favour of a spiritual self-reliance, limited only by its obligations to remake the public world, whose deceptions and inadequacies were rejected not in the name of privatism but of truth. But Baldwin inhabits a more sceptical world and his racial identity is forced to concede more power to social fictions than was that of the New England moralist.

In a sense, of course, America has always prided itself on its improvizational qualities, and in his essays Baldwin has repeatedly insisted on the parallel between the Negro in search of selfhood and the American intent on distilling a national identity. And he was clearly right in insisting on his American-ness. It is stamped on his imaginative enterprise. But the fluidities of the American system have historically not extended to the Negro. On this the country had been absolute. Where everything else has changed, to Baldwin this at least has remained a constant. And in this respect the experience of black and white is dissimilar. Certainly the irony of Baldwin claiming an American heritage in his early books of essays at the moment when facilities in southern towns, which he himself was not to visit until his early thirties, were still segregated, was not lost on his critics. Yet Baldwin's view was that though American identity and history had indeed been built on a denial of human complexity and freedom, this was a denial of an essential American idealism to which he wished to lay claim. His resistance to protest fiction (see "Everybody's Protest Novel") and, implicitly, to the naturalistic novel, lay precisely in the fact that it denied access to this idealism, that it made the self into a simple product of biological and environmental determinism. It denied the possibility of escape. And that, arguably, is at the heart of Baldwin's work: the need to forge a truce with determinism and with punishing social constraints, a truce which can sustain the individual even, perhaps, in face of the knowledge of its inevitable collapse. The escape to Europe is simply an attempt to create geographically that space for manoeuvre which in America has to be won through an exertion of imagination or will.

But the ironies emanating from his American identity were not simply those contained in the obvious dissonance between American idealism and reality. As he himself fully realized, his very articulateness is itself fraught with ambiguities which seem to nail him permanently to a paradoxical view of self and cultural identity. Indeed, Baldwin has always been aware of the special problem of language for the black writer. "It is quite possible to say that the price a Negro pays for becoming articulate is to find himself, at length, with nothing to be articulate about." The word becomes a barrier, indeed a protection, between the self and experience. The reduction of social event to language becomes in itself a form of escape. Initially, experience intervenes between the self and the articulation of that experience, but in turn language intervenes between the self and the experience. He is crushed from two directions.

"The root function of language," Baldwin suggests, "is to control the universe by describing it." But the black finds that access to language is not access to power, to control over his environment or himself. Language becomes disfunctional. Historically, of course, it betrayed him more fully into the power of those who sought to control him by offering means to facilitate that control. And once in possession of that language he becomes, perforce, heir to those very cultural presumptions to which he is formally denied free access. In turn he is then blessed or fated with a fluency which draws him steadily away from his own past. He is thus left with a cultural inheritance characterized by ambiguity, self-doubt and linguistic paradox. And Baldwin's work carries this mark. The personal pronoun, as he applies it, in *Nobody Knows My Name* and *Notes of a Native Son*, means sometimes Negro and sometimes American, a pronominal uncertainty which goes to the heart of that concern with identity which characterizes so many of his essays and so much of his work. And when he assumes an identification with his American self against his racial identity the effect is more ambivalent. For the cultural nationalists of the sixties his assertion that "Our dehumanization of the Negro . . . is indivisible from our dehumanization of ourselves: the loss of our identity is the price we pay for our annulment of his," is an expression of a desire for cultural assimilation which goes beyond a rhetorical device.

His rhetorical style, particularly that of the latter part of his career, is, in fact, a product of the battle to enforce his authority over language, to make it accommodate itself to an experience which it had been designed to justify and impose. As he put it, "you've simply got to force the language to pay attention to you in order to exist in it." The central problem, as he explained to Margaret Mead in 1970, was "how are we ever going to achieve some kind of language which will make my experience articulate to you and yours to me? Because you and I have been involved for all our lives . . . in some effort of translation."

Protest was implied in Baldwin's stance as an essayist. He was indeed a mediator, explaining the Negro to America by translating his experience into American terms, by establishing his own struggle for identity as of a kind with that of the American, anxious to distil meaning from history and experience. Like Ralph Ellison, he is essentially calling for the restoration of American idealism, and sees the route to that as lying through the individual: "An honest examination of the national life proves how far we are from the standard of human freedom with which we began. The recovery of this standard demands of everyone who loves this country a hard look at himself, for the greatest achievements must begin somewhere, and they always begin with the person."

His trip to Paris in 1948 was an American search for personal and national identity in an Old World which could render up an image of the New partly from its own desire to translate promise and threat into concrete form, and partly from its own ability to conceive of an America luminous with a meaning derived from those very contradictions which the American writer frequently found so disabling. In part, of course, it was the old game of discovering the limits of the self by abstracting it from the viscous world of its daily setting; it was an attempt to see what could survive such spiritual surgery—an act of definition by elimination, an attempt to find which conflicts were internal and definitional and which part of a dialectic between the unexamined self and the social projections of that self. For a black American it afforded the only opportunity to venture outside of the myth which defined him, and, in a curious way, protected him, insofar as it offered a self-image requiring only acceptance. Here, as Baldwin knew, he would be judged for himself, or at least in the context of other compulsions than the familiar ones. Yet it was as an American that he found himself responding, as an American that Europeans perceived him. And what he learned was the impossibility of distinguishing a clear line between the self and the culture in which that self develops. Once in Europe he felt as "American as any Texas GI," freed from the necessary reflexes which had once concealed his own identity from others and hence, eventually, from himself.

It was a move which sprang from the conviction that neither an unquestioned community of suffering, nor an assumed American homogeneity, offered a real clue to personal meaning. Baldwin wanted to find out "in what way the *specialness* of [his] experience could be made to connect [him] with other people instead of dividing [him] from them." And that specialness could only be abstracted by removing himself from a culture whose definitions of him sprang from compulsions shaped partly by history and partly by the pressure of a perverted puritanism and a hermeneutic of suffering and guilt.

"Everybody's Protest Novel" was not so much a necessary assault on a major icon of black literature as it was an expression of his desire to resist the role which he could feel being pressed upon him. To be a Negro writer was to be reduced to a socio-literary category. His subject was not just himself, in the sense that it always is for the writer, it was *himself as Negro*. And his assault on the protest novel was an attempt to create sufficient space for himself to operate, outside of the terms which it seemed his fate to embrace. As he said in the introduction to his early book of essays, *Notes of a Native Son*, "I have not written about being a Negro at such length because I expect that to be my only subject, but only because it was the gate I had to unlock before I could hope to write about anything else." At the beginning of his career, already writing his first novel, he felt the need to establish his own right to be seen outside the terms which seemed to mark the limits prescribed for the black novelist, by white society on the one hand, and by the moral demands of black suffering on the other.

He reacted against the Bigger Thomas of Richard Wright's *Native Son*, he admitted, partly because he seemed to him to represent a possibility which had to be rejected if he was to escape a self-destructive rage. In an early story called "Previous Condition," published in 1948, he displaces this violence into the imagination of his protagonist: "I wanted to kill her, I watched her stupid, wrinkled frightened white face and I wanted to take a club, a hatchet, and bring it down with all my weight, splitting her skull down the middle where she parted her iron-grey hair." But Baldwin is less interested in the literal discharge of hatred than in its power to distort the psyche, to warp personal and private history. It was precisely to escape such a distortion that he fled to Europe, a process which he describes in "This Morning, This Evening, So Soon," published in *Going to Meet the Man*, which remains one of his best stories and one which is crucial to an understanding of his position.

It concerns a black American actor/singer who lives in France with a Swedish woman, Harriet, and their son, and is in part an explanation of the sense of release which expatriation granted to him. For though he concedes a determining power to race, religion and nationality, the story is offered as evidence of the fact that such determinants are deadly if they are not transcended: "everyone's life begins on a level where races, armies, and churches stop." And the gift of expatriation is precisely such a transcendence, for it enables individuals to confront themselves and others outside of the constraining power of myth.

Black men and white women free themselves of a public rage and coercive power which, in America, would have become private compulsions. They are also free of a language which might otherwise throw its own reductive net around them. As the protagonist's sister observes, "Language is experience and language is power." The failure of black Americans, as she sees it, is that they employ a language of power which must be ironic since it is detached from their experience. And yet this, of course, is Baldwin's language too and the story can be seen as a confessional work of some honesty. For the protagonist recognizes that his success has in part been generated by a refusal to be identified too closely with the misery of his people, by associating himself, on the contrary, with those responsible for their suffering. It has also been dependent on his refusal to grant any ambiguity to French racial attitudes. France had removed the cataract from his eyes, with respect to America, at the cost of a moral myopia with regard to French attitudes.

A brief return to America reminds him that there his life is a concession offered to him by whites. But a conversation with his French director also reminds him that suffering is not a black prerogative. For he had lost a wife and son in the war and knows the weight of history as well as the black American. The real American sin is presented as an innocence of history, a failure to perceive that the past demands a price from the present. And this is a message which Baldwin himself felt increasingly obliged to underline as his career developed.

For Baldwin, Europe's function was precisely to release him from an identity which was no more than a projection of his racial inheritance. It was not, as LeRoi Jones was later to imply, that he wished to deny his colour but rather that he recognized the danger implicit in allowing public symbols of oppression or resistance to stand as adequate expressions of the self. As he said in his introduction to *Nobody Knows My Name*,

> In America, the color of my skin had stood between myself and me; in Europe, that barrier was down. Nothing is more desirable than to be released from an affliction, but nothing is more frightening than to be divested of a crutch. It turned out that the question of who I was was not solved because I had removed myself from the social forces which menaced me—anyway, those forces had become interior, and I had dragged them across the ocean with me. The question of who I was had at last become a personal question, and the answer was to be found in me.

For it was Baldwin's assumption that the question of colour, crucially important on a moral level, concealed a more fundamental problem, the problem of self. And it is in that sense that he felt most American.

But he negotiates a privileged position for himself by claiming an American identity (while naturally disavowing the guilt for a prejudice which he did not originate and for a history which he played no part in determining), and simultaneously embracing a Negro identity (while declining the cultural temporizing and disabling pathology which he otherwise identifies as the natural inheritance of the black American). Both American and Negro search endlessly for identity. Only Baldwin, in the eye of the storm, realizes that it resides in stillness, in an acceptance, not of injustice nor of public roles, but of the authenticity of the self. His failure lies in his inability to reveal the authenticating process at work. Sexuality is clearly a part of it; in some way, supposedly, it tells the truth that the intellect denies. It offers a vital clue, he feels, both to the American need to dramatize innocence and to the real roots of prejudice. In his essay "Nobody Knows My Name," he coyly hints that desegregation battles have to do with "political power and . . . with sex." Now, on an obvious level, he is clearly right. It was certainly never an argument about educational theories. But the link between that observation and the obsessive question of identity is not so clear. Meanwhile his own sexual ambiguity was itself a confusing factor, acceptance for him meaning the difficult task of accepting the real nature of his bisexuality, abandoning illusion for reality.

On the face of it the American problem with regard to sex was somewhat different. It was that sexuality had so often been presented as an absolute, as a metaphor for evil or anarchy, or, alternatively, utopian bliss, that it could not be so easily integrated into a realistic model of society. Its metaphoric weight was simply too great. But for Baldwin acceptance implied precisely that elevation of sex into metaphor, so that in virtually all of his work it stands either as an image of exploitation and abuse, or of an innocence with the power to transform social reality: sex as weapon, sex as redemption. In other words he is never more American than in his symbolic perception of sexuality, and what he presents as a kind of emotional realism is in fact a familiar form of sentimentality. It can be found just as easily in Hemingway, in Tennessee Williams, and in Norman Mailer and is no more sophisticated there, except that Mailer, whom Baldwin actually attacked for his sentimentality, purports to see sex as a dialectical term. Baldwin, in struggling to escape the sexual myths which surround the Negro in America, has simply succumbed to others.

He suggests that Wright placed violence where sex should have been, because he was unable to analyse the real nature of the rage which he perceived; but Baldwin himself endows sex with a brutal physicality which is in effect a simple transposition of social violence. Having claimed in his essays that it is principal, in his novels he presents it as agent, while the ambiguities of sexual contact, in part an expression of self, in part a surrender of self, in part aggression, in part submission, become an enactment of the ambivalence implied in the self's confrontation with society and the tensions of racial relationships. For if in suppressing the Negro, white Americans were in fact "burying . . . the unspeakably dark, guilty, erotic past which the Protestant fathers made him bury," then the release of that erotic self should serve to heal the wound opened up by that denial of the whole man. And Baldwin was by no means alone in this assumption. What he adds is the presumption that the existence of the Negro has facilitated this disruption of identity, that he has collaborated in a myth of black sexual potency. The risk is that in releasing this sexuality in his own work he is in danger of endorsing the metaphoric presumptions of those Protestant fathers or, as bad, generating a false image of reconciliation.

In a graceless essay called "Alas, Poor Richard," following Richard Wright's death, he asserted that "the war in the breast between blackness and whiteness which caused Richard such pain, need not be a war. It is a war which just as it denies both the heights and the depths of our natures, takes, and has taken visibly and invisibly, as many white lives as black ones." For him, Wright was "among the most illustrious victims of this war." Borrowing one of Wright's favourite phrases, he had, he suggested, wandered in a no-man's-land between black and white. The act of reconciliation simply lay beyond Wright's imagination. But what, then, does Baldwin offer? Only, it appears, the fact that whiteness has lost its power and that blackness will soon do so. Thus the crucial act of reconciliation will take place in the moral sensibility of the Negro. But to be made flesh, however, it must assume a reality beyond that privileged environment. And the only way in which he can dramatize it is in the literal embrace of black and white, a coition which, like that implied, but mercifully not enacted, at the end of Hawthorne's *The House of the Seven Gables*, will produce a moral synthesis. The trouble is that, for Baldwin, history cannot be so easily propitiated by simple images of sexual union.

For Baldwin, society is bound together by fear of our unknown selves. In other words, he offers us a neat reversal of the Lockean model. Men form society not to protect their freedom but to evade it. The notion is a Freudian one, so it is perhaps not surprising that the force he invokes to neutralize this process in his work is sexuality. This becomes the key to a real sense of community. The sentimentality of such a conviction is clear and may account for the real evasions which are to be found at the heart of so much of his own work. For social evil is thus seen as deriving from a desire for order and a fear of "our unknown selves . . . which can save us—'from the evil that is

in the world.' " Indeed by this logic the victim creates himself by accepting
the need for social structure and granting it his acquiescence, when all the time
"our humanity is our burden, our life; we need not battle for it; we need only
to do what is infinitely more difficult—that is, accept it."

In the case of his attack on *Native Son*, he is offering a severe misreading,
for far from being trapped within sociological generalizations, far from reducing
complexity to simplicity and failing to engage the dangerous but liberating
freedom of the individual, the genuinely subversive quality of that novel lies
not in its attack on American society but in its conviction that individual action
and the individual mind are not socially determined or socially bound. It is
true that Wright's novel was a curiously schizophrenic work, with the
individualistic drive of the narrative operating against an adjectival insistence
on constriction and the deterministic weight implied by its sectional headings:
Fear, Flight, Fate. It is equally true that, if events constitute successive stages
in the liberation of the sensibility, they are also, by inverse law, stages in the
diminishing world of social possibilities. But Baldwin was saddled with the same
paradox. He wishes to presume both that the self is real and pre-social, and
that it cannot exist apart from its determinants. The result is a curious and
distinctive tension between what he sees as an American sensibility and a free-
ranging existential self—yet another example of his Manichean imagination
which sees himself as the product of the Old World and the New, black and
white, vengeance and love, male and female, probing intellect and liberating
imagination. It is a dialectical process of which the self is the putative synthesis.
And, to Baldwin, this is an American process.

To Baldwin, the objective of the novelist is to serve truth, which he defines
as "a devotion to the human being, his freedom and fulfilment." To see the
individual as only an image of a race is to exchange reality for symbol, a life
for a cause. And this was the real target of "Everybody's Protest Novel"—the
retreat into metaphor. And just as Moby Dick was not to be understood either
as type or as emblem, so the individual's reality lies outside his availability as
public symbol. Baldwin could already feel the pressure of the public role he
was inevitably offered and which he felt the need to resist. "What is today
offered as his [the black writer's] Responsibility," he said, "is, when he believes
it, his corruption and our loss." Curiously, *Native Son*'s vulnerability to Baldwin's
criticism lay less in the element of protest, which is the source of its central
ambiguity, than in the vague mythologizing of the social impulse which Bigger
Thomas feels. The edge of his newly discovered identity blurs at the very
moment of its coalescence. Baldwin suggests that American uncertainty about
identity, and American disregard for the identity of others, derive from a
contempt for history and historical process. Doubtful of historical logic, the

American has tended to distrust time and to value experience – to assume that identity therefore is the product of events outside of time. A name is no more than the emblem of a man until it is claimed in action. The result is a social formlessness which masquerades as freedom but actually smacks of anarchy. And this breeds a Hemingwayesque pragmatic morality which is as likely to validate racism as anything else. It is, he suggests, an American confusion to think that it is possible to consider the person apart from all the forces which have produced him, since American history turns on the abstraction of the individual from his social and cultural setting. And yet this is precisely Baldwin's assumption, since, as we have seen above, when it serves his purpose he too posits the existence of a primary self outside of and unaffected by history. This, indeed, is a clue to a basic contradiction in his position which enables him both to use the moral self to indict the social world and the social world to explain the collapse of self.

The recurring pain to which Baldwin avers is the alienation from self and from the cultural experience of the Negro, an alienation which is not neutralized by expatriation, as this intensifies the guilt and adds a further level of ambiguity since now he must battle for possession of an American identity which, if the source of his pain, is also the key to its transcendence. As he puts it in a 1950 essay, "Encounter on the Seine,"

> To accept the reality of his being an American becomes a matter
> involving his integrity and his greatest hopes, for only by accepting
> this reality can he hope to make articulate to himself or to others
> the uniqueness of his experience, and to set free the spirit so long
> anonymous and caged.

More than this, like Wright, he felt that the black experience not merely offered a clue to American moral ambiguity but that it functioned as metaphor, that "in white Americans he finds reflected – repeated, as it were, in a higher key – his tensions, his terrors, his tenderness" and that "in this need to establish himself in relation to his past he is most American, that this depthless alienation from oneself and one's people is, in sum, the American experience."

Having previously argued, in his essay on the protest novel, against metaphoric reductivism, he now strains, as expatriate, to transform his own experience into an emblem of dispossession in precisely the same way that Wright had done in a series of works starting with *Native Son* and running through "The Man Who Lived Underground" and *The Outsider*. Where he does try to establish a distinction it is that between the social and the metaphysical image, yet this is a distinction which he finds it difficult to sustain. It now turns out that his real rejection of Wright's novel lies in what he takes

to be the inaccuracy of its portrait, in its faulty sociology, a conviction that
the problem is being engaged too soon, at a level which denies not so much
the complexity of the Negro, as that of an essential human nature. For he
feels that "the battle is elsewhere. It proceeds far from us in the heat and horror
and pain of life itself where all men are betrayed by greed and guilt and blood
lust and where no man's hands are clean." It remains unexamined since, as
Camus realized, the logic of this position is that if all men are guilty then all
men are innocent. If the sociological approach implies the possibility of facile
solutions then assertions of an immutable human nature, generating social action,
leave one with the sentimentalities of evil and innocence, with desperate images
such as that which concludes but scarcely resolves Steinbeck's *The Grapes of
Wrath*, in which social realities are invited to defer before the reassertion of
human goodness. For this was a paradox he was not ready to engage, indeed
has never engaged, since he has continued to dramatize human action as a
battle between good and evil, a battle which he believes to characterize American
political and cultural presumptions. Out of the sociological frying pan and into
the metaphysical fire. Knowing that "anyone who insists on remaining in a
state of innocence long after that innocence is dead, turns himself into a monster,"
his puritan mentality continues to play with Manichean ideas.

The essence of his contradictions was exposed very effectively in a
conversation between Baldwin and Margaret Mead which took place in 1970 — a
discussion in which the anthropologist acts as a useful restraining influence
on the writer's sentimentalities and on his increasingly casual use of language.
Baldwin was intent on establishing an historical guilt, incurred by the act of
enslavement, but inherited by white Americans of the present. In this respect,
he admitted himself to be something of an Old Testament prophet. But he
also wished to offer the possibility of absolution, and the resultant contradiction
between an ineradicable guilt and a necessary grace, which has characterized
so much of his work, was carefully exposed by Margaret Mead. Speaking of
the process of enslavement of blacks, he describes it as "the crime which is
spoken of in the Bible, the sin against the Holy Ghost which cannot be forgiven." The exchange which followed reveals his tendency to let language and
imagery outstrip his convictions:

MEAD: Then we've nowhere to go.
BALDWIN: No, we have atonement.
MEAD: Not for the sin against the Holy Ghost.
BALDWIN: No?
MEAD: I mean, after all, you were once a theologian. . . . And the
    point about the sin against the Holy Ghost is that —

BALDWIN: Is that it cannot be forgiven.

MEAD: So if you state a crime as impossible of forgiveness you've doomed everyone.

BALDWIN: No. I don't think I was as merciless as the Old Testament prophets. But I do agree with Malcolm X, that sin demands atonement.

MEAD: Whose sin? I mean, you're making racial guilt—

BALDWIN: No.

MEAD: Yes. You are.

BALDWIN: I'm not talking about race. I'm talking about the fact.

MEAD: But you are. . . . You're taking an Old Testament position, that the sins of the fathers are visited on their children.

BALDWIN: They are.

MEAD: The consequences are visited on the children.

BALDWIN: It's the same thing, isn't it?

MEAD: No, it's not the same thing at all. Because it's one thing to say, All right, I'm suffering for what my fathers did—

BALDWIN: I don't mean that, I don't mean that! I don't mean that at all! I mean something else! I mean something which I may not be able to get to . . .

MEAD: . . . but when you talk about atonement you're talking about people who weren't *born* when this was committed.

BALDWIN: No. I mean the recognition of where one finds oneself in time or history or now. . . . After all, I'm not guiltless, either. I sold my brothers or my sisters—

MEAD: When did you?

BALDWIN: Oh, a thousand years ago, it doesn't make any difference.

MEAD: It *does* make a difference. I think if one takes that position it's absolutely hopeless. I will *not* accept any guilt for what anybody else did. I will accept guilt for what I did myself.

Jean-Paul Sartre makes a similar point in *Anti-Semite and Jew* when he observes that "if one is going to reproach little children for the sins of their grandfathers, one must first of all have a very primitive conception of what constitutes responsibility."

What Baldwin's comments to Margaret Mead demonstrate is a desire, evident throughout his published works, to present history as present reality, to establish a social responsibility which, because he chooses to dramatize it in terms of sin and guilt, he is unable to establish as an active principle. The Old Testament prophet denies the efficacy of New Testament grace. The writer who wishes to establish a racial indictment is thus inhibited from dramatizing the need for racial reconciliation which is a conviction which he holds with equal force. His desire to establish his belief that individuals are responsible moral creatures is simultaneously undermined by his conviction that their crime is ineradicable and human beings ineluctably wicked. The problem does not reside in language alone, but in his own terrible ambivalences which lead him to accuse and defend, condemn and rescue with equal conviction. The deficiency is an intellectual one.

Even now, in one mood, he sees a solution in some kind of symbolic union of black and white for which he can find no historic justification and for which he can establish no social mechanism. When asked, some twenty-five years after his first essay, how he meant to go about securing his solution to the problem, his reply was simply "I don't know yet." And then, slipping into the opposite mood, which has always been the other side to this sentimental vision, he offered the only solution which he could see: "Blow it up."

STEPHEN ADAMS

Giovanni's Room:
The Homosexual as Hero

"I think that I know something about the American masculinity which most men of my generation do not know because they have not been menaced by it in the way that I have been," declares James Baldwin in "The Black Boy Looks at the White Boy." The male homosexual is also menaced by definitions of manhood that are used to denigrate his existence and individual dignity. Baldwin is passionately involved with the problems of both racism and homosexuality, so that his portrayal of racial conflict within a society often lends special authority to his analysis of that society's sexual stereotypes, and vice versa. He testifies to the difficulties of achieving a satisfying personal identity in a society which superimposes its conceptions of *the* negro or *the* homosexual upon individuals and which creates false images of people only to persecute them with those same images.

Baldwin's identification with these minorities has sometimes brought his status as an artist into question; to regard him as a "black writer" or as a "homosexual writer" is to suggest limits on his individuality and on his treatment of his chosen subject matter. Such labelling underlines the tenacity of the very stereotypes Baldwin fights. A racial or a sexual identity which does not coincide with that of the majority is frequently presumed to disqualify a writer from entering into territories beyond that minority experience. In *After the Lost Generation* (1951), John W. Aldridge pontificates on the nature of the "homosexual talent" and concludes: "it can develop in only one direction, and it can never take the place of the whole range of human experience." In *The Literary Situation* (1954), Malcolm Cowley amuses himself with references to the arrival

From *The Homosexual as Hero in Contemporary Fiction.* © 1980 by Stephen Adams. Vision Press Limited, 1980. Originally entitled "James Baldwin."

of the "fairy-Freudian" novel and wonders whether the homosexual writer who attempts to portray "normal passions" can never do so without transposing the sexes or indulging in spiteful malice. *Giovanni's Room*, which deals with the affair between David, a white American, and Giovanni, an Italian, has called forth critical comments which illustrate the reductive implications of the "black writer" label. In *The Return of the Vanishing American* (1968) Leslie Fiedler remarks that "one suspects Baldwin's Giovanni of being a Negro disguised as a European, and the book consequently of being a disguised Southern." On the other hand, G. M. Sarotte would have us believe that David is the Harlem Negro in disguise – the author in a blond wig, in fact, taking a holiday from himself. It is doubtless only a matter of time before these insights are pieced together as proof of the narcissism of the "homosexual writer."

When heterosexual prejudice joins forces with racial convictions, as in Eldridge Cleaver's essay "Notes on a Native Son" (in *Soul on Ice*, 1968), then the complexity of the individual writer's work is lost in a set of emotional generalisations. Cleaver, for whom homosexuality is a "sickness" on a level with "baby-rape," attacks Baldwin by likening him to the black homosexual who, deprived of his masculinity by worship of the white man, turns his self-contempt on other blacks, whilst fawning on his white lover. Cleaver colludes in the white man's myth of the Negro's sexual potency, to dismiss the black homosexual as a traitor, a carrier of some white "disease." Clearly, the knowledge Baldwin claims of American masculinity – as one who has been menaced by it – has an authority which in turn menaces preferred images of manhood, both black and white. He puzzles over his own definitions in ways which explode the notions of narrowness in the experience of a racial or sexual minority. The Negro or the homosexual are, in his analysis, "inventions" which reveal, ironically, more about the workings of mainstream culture. Just as he portrays the Negro in a manner which challenges White America to take stock of itself, so the heterosexual confronted with his "blackening" of the outcast homosexual can be brought to greater self-awareness. This is made satirically explicit in his remark:

> People invent categories in order to feel safe. White people invented
> black people to give white people identity. . . . Straight cats invent
> faggots so they can sleep with them without becoming faggots
> themselves.

In their various ways Baldwin's first four novels reflect the difficulties of individuals for whom the question of personal identity – because of their psychic make-up, colour, or sexuality – bears an urgent relation to that of social survival. *Go Tell It on the Mountain* (1953) and *Giovanni's Room* (1956) explore the extent to which inner drives can be contained within the available, approved models of identity. In the first novel, John Grimes strives to sublimate his adolescent sexual confusion, his rebelliousness, and his fears of the brutal Harlem ghetto with its encircling white world, within the traditional sanctuary of the church. David, the white protagonist of the second novel, seeks a refuge in the conventional, outward trappings of manhood in a vain attempt to exorcise his homosexual longings. Both novels dramatise mechanisms of self-betrayal and the sacrifice of personal fulfilment to the gods of conformity. *Another Country* (1962) and *Tell Me How Long the Train's Been Gone* (1968) deal with characters who rebel against the destiny society would prescribe for them, though not all survive to give that rebellion meaningful form. In *Another Country* failures in love are redeemed through a pattern of atonement whereby the characters commit themselves to personal relationships which defy social prejudice, whilst the tone of the later novel is angrier, in keeping with its wider focus on a rebellion which reaches out from individual lives across the whole social and political plane.

Of all Baldwin's novels, least attention is paid to *Giovanni's Room*. Most frequently it is dismissed as thinly disguised autobiography or condemned for an alleged narrowness of theme and treatment. The first-person confessional style naturally encourages the view of David as Baldwin's surrogate, and given the autobiographical nature of *Go Tell It on the Mountain* and that like his protagonist Baldwin had turned to Europe in search of greater personal freedom, it is perhaps inevitable that, like *The City and the Pillar*, this novel should have been misconstrued as a "lurid memoir." Undoubtedly it draws heavily upon the author's own experience, but this does not justify its relegation to the category of "unprocessed raw material of art"—which is how Robert Bone has described it. The confessional style is the necessary expression of David's character and situation and it is unfair to ignore Baldwin's conscious artistic intention and to treat his hero simply as a vehicle for psychoanalytical speculation on his author's own sexual dilemma.

David is successfully presented as a representative white American, one whose experiences dramatise the thesis Baldwin expounds in "A Question of Identity" (1954), regarding a particular generation of young Americans drawn to the bohemian life in Paris, "the city where everyone loses his head, and his morals, lives through at least one *histoire d'amour* . . . and thumbs his nose at the Puritans." But as this surfeit of freedom unnerves the traveller, "he begins to long for the prison of home—home then becoming the place where questions are not asked." David fits into this pattern, attempting at all costs to preserve his "innocence," a quality Baldwin associates specifically with white Americans. In the essay "The Black Boy Looks at the White Boy," he argues:

> The things that most white people imagine they can salvage from
> the storm of life is really, in sum, their innocence. . . . I am afraid
> that most of the white people I have ever known impressed me
> as being in the grip of a weird nostalgia, dreaming of a vanished
> state of security and order.

In David's case, "innocence" is a version of himself he wishes to recover as
a defence against the guilty secret of his homosexual drives; although he goes
to Paris, typically, to "find" himself, what he hopes to discover are proofs of
his innocence. A tourist on a psychological level, he flirts with the gay underworld to persuade himself that his "home" is not there. However, his sense
of his identity is shattered when he falls in love with the Italian barman,
Giovanni, and he makes a last desperate bid to secure himself from homosexual
guilt by committing himself to his relationship with an American girl, Hella.

Far from constituting a self-indulgent fictionalised memoir, narrow in theme
and treatment, *Giovanni's Room* stands in ironic relation to that genre perfected
by Henry James, where the American innocent is put to the test of experience
in the Old World. Indeed, it is a genre which continues to be redefined in
homosexual terms, as is evident in the work of another American writer, Donald
Windham. His novel *Two People* (1965) deals with the love affair between
Forrest, a young American business man, temporarily estranged from his wife,
and Marcello, a seventeen-year-old Italian youth living in Rome, who is
undergoing a crisis in his relations with his family. Their affair is presented
as a stage in self-discovery; it offers a refuge from their problems, a basis from
which to reappraise their need for the "closeness and security" of their respective
homes, and (perhaps unrealistically) it allows each to develop or to resume
heterosexual relationships with a new confidence.

David and Hella exemplify the process Baldwin discerns in the experience
of fellow American expatriates. Both, ostensibly, dedicate themselves to a quest
for personal identity through sexual freedom and the bohemian life, but when
this raises questions which are too threatening they seek refuge in convention,
looking backwards to America to restore some sense of order and security in
their lives. Reflecting on the "peculiar innocence and confidence" of their early
nights of "fun," David admits that "nothing is more unbearable, once one has
it, than freedom. I suppose this was why I asked her to marry me: to give
myself something to be moored to." Hella arrives at a similar conclusion. She
is a student of painting until she realises her lack of talent and is ready to throw
herself in the Seine, she thinks of herself as a modern, independent woman
until the novelty of promiscuity palls and commitment to someone like David
seems the only alternative. There is little evidence of passion in their relationship

and marriage is a calculated choice. On her return from Spain where she had gone to consider David's proposal, Hella communicates in clichéd terms which betray her apologetic retreat into convention and her lack of genuine feeling. She does not want to "miss the boat" and, like all good heroines, she confesses, "I'm not really the emancipated girl I try to be at all. I guess I just want a man to come home to me every night. . . . I want to start having babies. In a way, it's really all I'm good for." Her fears of not being a "real" woman coincide with David's fears of not being a "real" man. He feels as if he had fallen out of some "web of safety" and longs to be on the inside again, "with my manhood unquestioned, watching my woman putting my children to bed." The "innocence" the American couple seek to preserve is juxtaposed with the sufferings of Giovanni. His despair underlines the self-indulgence of their fears of "missing the boat," their "fun," their fashionable existentialism and their suicidal fancies.

The framework of David's relationships with Hella and with Giovanni is underpinned by religious and metaphysical dimensions which are suggested by the comment Jacques makes when David tells him how he wishes that Giovanni could have stayed happily in Italy and sung his life away. "Nobody can stay in the garden of Eden . . . I wonder why," Jacques remarks. The question continues to haunt David who reflects that if everyone has their own Eden, "they have scarcely seen their garden before they see the flaming sword. Then, perhaps, life only offers the choice of remembering the garden or forgetting it. Either, or: it takes strength to remember, it takes another kind of strength to forget, it takes a hero to do both." The passage crystallizes the novel's underlying dialogue of extremes: innocence and guilt, heaven and hell, cleanliness and dirt, ideal love and perfunctory sex.

Both David and Giovanni have their own private memory of an Eden, and the sword which bars their return. David remembers his adolescent love for his best friend, Joey, and the idyllic summer weekend they spent alone together. The morning after a playful wrestling match had turned into ecstatic lovemaking, David's puritan conscience had struck such fear and remorse into him that the "beautiful creation" of Joey's body, for which his body still longed, became "the black opening of a cavern . . . in which I would lose my manhood." From then on, David had been a stranger to himself, his father and to all around him. He willed himself to forget Joey, he buried his sense of guilt and battened down the hatches on his psyche. Where Giovanni is concerned, expulsion from Eden came when the girl he loved in his home village gave birth to his grey, twisted, dead son. As in the case of David, it was as if life had played him a cruel trick to put his manhood in question. He had raged against this treachery, spat on the crucifix, and walked out for good on his girl, his family and his

village. Both men had taken refuge in an extreme attitude to life. Giovanni
surrendered himself to the "dirty world," to despair, as if to do penance for
his sins; David had run away from what Giovanni later describes as the "stink
of love," in order to safeguard his purity and moral "cleanliness." But through
their love for each other, they are given the chance to abandon their narrow
philosophies, to end their self-imposed exiles, to enter into what Baldwin insists
upon as the necessary dialectic of joy and pain in any relationship, and so to
make a "home" for themselves in the world.

For David, the "dirty world" from which he seeks to dissociate himself
is symbolised by the homosexual milieu into which his friend, Jacques,
occasionally introduces him. If indeed that world is "dirty," then David's attitudes
and behaviour help to make it so. His efforts to prove to himself and to the
company of Guillaume's bar that he does not "belong" are such that we share
Jacques' relish at the moment when David's *"immaculate* manhood" is com-
promised by his evident attraction to the new barman, Giovanni. Until then,
the American has been the picture of unsullied heterosexuality, enjoying the
envy he arouses, and bolstering up his sense of his own masculinity by the
process Baldwin refers to elsewhere as the "invention" of "faggots." David, who
exploits Jacques' loneliness and despises Guillaume, sneers at the inmates of
this "peacock garden" which "sounded like a barnyard" – a caricature of that
lost Eden.

If the gay underworld seems squalid and shameful, this is not depicted
as any exclusive concomitant of homosexuality. Hella's account of the pensioned
widows in Spain ogling anything in trousers, and David's abuse of the American
girl, Sue, to convince himself of his continued ability to "perform," demonstrate
a complementary lovelessness in the heterosexual world. Furthermore, David's
contempt for the homosexual milieu indicates his failure to understand and
to see beyond the promiscuity to the pain of someone like Jacques. Jacques,
like a mentor, seeks to make David face up to his own involvement in meaningless sex and recommends him to think of those encounters when he
"pretended nothing was happening down there in the dark." If Jacques' life
is shameful, then it is partly because of those who like David are too ashamed
to love.

Giovanni is presented as the living example of Jacques' conviction that
homosexuality is not in itself "dirty." He is encountered *within* that underworld, his dignity, freshness and vitality framed by the gaudy antics of its inmates
and their sordid dramas of prostitution – like a figure in a religious icon, with
"all the light of that gloomy tunnel trapped around his head." Jacques voices
Baldwin's positive philosophy of homosexual love when he urges David to seize
his opportunity for happiness: "you can make your time together anything

but dirty . . . if you will *not* be ashamed, if you will only *not* play it safe." Given the contrast between the customers of Guillaume's bar and the two heroes, one might expect their love affair to be idealised. Indeed, for the author sympathetic to homosexuality, the temptation must be to disprove the death of Romantic literature since any pair of homosexual lovers has an inbuilt potential for a dramatic, if not tragic, destiny. But with the exception of the bright haloes and starry-eyed fatality of their encounter (Giovanni's eyes actually are "unbelievably like morning stars"), Baldwin depicts the more complex reality of such a relationship and it is unfair to accuse him, as does Irving Howe, of "whipped cream sentimentalism" whenever he deals with homosexual love.

The first flush of passion is quickly put to the test of everyday living by the need to give their relationship some framework other than the walls of Giovanni's room. Though David, with his economic security, feels the burden of Giovanni's salvation to be on him, it is clear that Giovanni has the more onerous task of rescuing David from the workings of sexual shame. The Italian's frankness, warmth and uninhibited desires are set against the other's duplicity, reserve and feelings of guilt. These differences form part of a cultural dialectic, the Mediterranean temperament being pitted against the North American in a confrontation between pagan and puritan outlooks on life. Whereas Giovanni is ready to scorn the "dirty words" that David's countrymen would apply to their situation, the latter is crippled by conventional morality. David tells himself: "The beast which Giovanni had awakened in me would never go to sleep again; but one day I would not be with Giovanni any more. And would I then, like all the others, find myself turning and following all kinds of boys down God knows what dark avenues, into what dark places?", revealing a fondness for melodrama and self-pity.

Giovanni's room comes to symbolise all the complex facets of their situation, and not, as Colin MacInnes supposes, "the sterility and self-destruction of homosexual love." At the outset, the room is a sanctuary from prying eyes and life there seems idyllic, out of time, as if it were taking place beneath the sea. But, for David, as Hella's return becomes imminent, the dimensions of the room shrink, it seems claustrophobic, a trap, an interrogation chamber. It has become a waiting room, where time hangs like a sword threatening to fall—anticipating those separate rooms where David and Giovanni will wait under the shadow of the guillotine. In retrospect, David, who attempted to think of it always as *Giovanni's* room, admits that it is like every room in which he has ever been or ever will be. That is to say, he is trapped in his own compartmentalised ways of thinking, in the prison of his own flesh.

David thinks of the dirt and debris in the room as a token of Giovanni's "regurgitated life," not just a matter of temperament but of "punishment and grief." Thus the room suggests more than the material shape of Giovanni's poverty, it is a chosen hell, a sign of his refusal to take responsibility for his own life and of his surrender to despair. It is a plea to David to transform his corner of that "dirty world." As David remarks, "I understood why Giovanni had wanted me and had brought me to his last retreat. I was to destroy this room and give to Giovanni a new and better life." The transient feel of the room is contrasted with the idea of "home" in the novel and with the desire to translate temporary sexual relationships into secure commitments. But David, a tourist to the last, will work only to make his stay more congenial. And though he resents playing "housewife" to Giovanni the "breadwinner," in reality David is the one with the means for them to leave the room and transform their situation. He tells himself he is right to abandon Giovanni by projecting his fears of a lasting homosexual commitment upon the room itself: it is a *maid's* room, squalid and dirty, echoing his view of the underworld and the "black cavern" which seems once more to be closing in on his precious manhood. It even has its own mocking reminder of the realm he has forsaken; on the wall is the image of a lady in a hoop skirt and a man in knee breeches, perpetually walking together in a garden of roses. When his father's letters ("Dear Butch . . . ") and finally Hella's return combine in urging him to "come home," he loses his nerve, repeats his adolescent flight from Joey, from the "stink of love"—and also from its redeeming possibilities.

The two men regress to their separate spheres: Giovanni to squalor and despair, David to salvage his "purity" and to "cleanse" himself. But like Giovanni, David enters into an artificial hell of his own making—as the name of his fiancée intimates. Giovanni once told him, "You don't have a home until you leave it and then, when you have left it, you can never go back." David is fated to bear witness to this comment for when he is reunited with Hella, it is "like a familiar darkened room in which I fumbled to find the light," an ironic reversal of his earlier longing to be safe in a lighted room with his manhood unquestioned and his woman putting his children to bed. Furthermore, his sad realisation that Giovanni's room was where he really belonged is framed by the novel's recurrent image of him in the deserted rooms of the house in the south of France where, abandoned by Hella, he cleans away the last traces of his presence.

In his essay "The Male Prison" (included in *Nobody Knows My Name*), Baldwin criticises Gide for separating sex and love in his life, for the irresponsibility of his homosexuality and his attempt to have his pleasures without "paying" for them. Similarly, David contrives to escape the responsibilities of his sexual love, to obtain for himself temporary pleasures. In the same essay, Baldwin also states that today's homosexual "can only save himself by the most tremendous exertion of all his forces from falling into an underworld in which he never meets either men or women, where it is impossible to have either a lover or a friend, where the possibility of genuine human involvement has altogether ceased." This passage touches upon the dilemma of both his characters. Giovanni casts himself to this underworld, to be used and defiled by it until, as once before, a passionate gesture of defiance seals his fate; in the past he spat on the crucifix, now he murders Guillaume, the symbolic lord of this "dirty" realm. David reaches his impasse by a different route: fleeing from love and its suffering he becomes, in Giovanni's words, "a lover who is neither man nor woman, nothing that I can ever know or touch," a prophecy confirmed by Hella when she eventually finds David in a gay bar. However, Giovanni's death is the ritual sacrifice which saves David from the "male prison," the tragic source of his self-knowledge and ultimately the catharsis from which a real spiritual purification can be hoped for. The long night of penance which shapes the novel, is an agonising endorsement of the love for Giovanni that he once sought to deny and more especially of Baldwin's own belief in the paradoxical beauty and dignity of suffering. David attempts the heroic role of bringing himself both to remember and to forget his garden of Eden—and so he walks off into the morning with "a dreadful weight of hope."

JAMES A. SNEAD

Baldwin Looks Back

It may well be that 40 years from now James Baldwin will be called the finest American essayist of his generation. He has certainly been, over the last 40 years, the most prolific and most durable. The patented Baldwin style—comma-filled and intricately digressive with its asides, refinements, anecdotes, sudden tirades—builds over time into an almost Pentecostal routine of internal "call-and-response." With the appearance of *The Price of the Ticket*, the American reader can now reassess a body of writing that, better than any other, looks back on the stormy relations between white and black America from 1948 to 1985.

Baldwin's literary career has been marked by a tension "between (his) life as a writer and (his) life as—not spokesman exactly, but as a public witness to the situation of black people." Baldwin's enormous popular success (his worldwide sales, running into the millions, make him easily the best-selling black writer of our time) is mainly a result of his fiction (*Giovanni's Room, Another Country*). But this volume of collected essays comprises a body of writing more direct in its aim, more coherent in its approach, and ultimately more convincing in its execution, than the fictional works by which Baldwin is usually known; some of these essays deserve attention as masterpieces, not just of social analysis, but of expository form. Baldwin is a bright angel, alerting us in urgent tones to a spiritual self-destruction already evident in America.

The 52 essays collected here (all published previously, except for the "Introduction") span a period of 37 years, a time of unprecedented social ferment. The collection includes all of Baldwin's key essays, detailing his progress from

From *Los Angeles Times* (December 1, 1985). © 1985 by The Times–Mirror Co.

the relative optimism of the fifties and sixties, to a bleaker militancy in the
seventies, to a somewhat mystical concern in the eighties with future generations,
"how to save our children." (The collection, unfortunately, omits the crucial
article on "Mass Culture and the Creative Artist.")

Baldwin writes in the tradition of Montaigne, Emerson and Thoreau: His
speculations never stray too far from autobiographical details. His "I" also (like
the narrator of Ellison's *Invisible Man*) describes the "you." Baldwin invites us
as readers to see ourselves mirrored in his inner states. With a blend of precision
and extravagance unmatched in modern American essayists, Baldwin's eye
documents exciting yet exacting times.

The fact is that Baldwin has seen and suffered much more than most—
and has survived to tell the tale. His sheer ubiquity is amazing: In one extended
recollection, *No Name in the Street*, we find Baldwin dodging racist policemen
in Montgomery and Little Rock, writing in Beverly Hills a stillborn screen
treatment of Malcolm X's autobiography, trading obscene oaths with a school
chum over a Harlem fried-chicken dinner, visiting a wrongly accused black
friend in a Hamburg prison, dining at the London Hilton with his British
publishers. He seems to have been nearly everywhere, done nearly everything,
and understood nearly everyone, from the lowliest chauffeur to highest
luminaries of politics and culture.

Baldwin has kept up a love/hate affair with Europe, but he has never been
far from American artistic life. He has known the likes of Richard Wright,
Chester Himes, William Styron, Norman Mailer. Returning to America in
1957 for an extended period, Baldwin became the moral scribe of "that betrayed
and co-opted insurrection that American folklore has trivialized into 'the civil
rights movement' "—he remains its most faithful witness. Indeed, his cameo
portraits of Martin Luther King, Jr., Medgar Evers and Malcolm X are definitive
examples of their genre.

Baldwin's essays present three basic stances: (1) Baldwin, the artist/solitary,
the *picaro* or outlaw whose behavior places him on the periphery of social
definition and sanction; (2) Baldwin, the penitent sinner, whose confession also
becomes our own; and (3) Baldwin, the prophetic visionary (a sort of latter-
day Amos, critical of the present, prescient about the future). Both his con-
fessorial and prophetic stances underpin Baldwin's basically evangelical quest,
despite his open break with the church as a youth.

Already in his first essay, "The Harlem Ghetto" (1948), we see that Baldwin
cannot abide the easy platitudes and sterile subterfuges that cloak the truth
of racial oppression. His exceptional candor is only possible because he has
scrutinized himself. Baldwin has, more than any other writer of his generation,
captivated the (normally white) American reader by speaking both as victimized

and victimizer, exposing racism from within as economic and psychological self-interest.

Baldwin sees his role as unmasking the central delusions that white Americans still hold about blacks. Racial interaction in America, he says, fetters blacks with pervasive reproofs, and misleads whites into a false sense of superiority. "The price of the ticket" to such deceptive comfort is high, in psychological, economic, ethical and historical terms. Whites see the false front blacks present as "good racial relations." White Americans, to the extent that they accept the role of "white man," are controlled by the history they have repressed: "They are, in effect, still trapped in a history which they do not understand; and until they understand it, they cannot be released from it." "Incoherence" takes the place of morality: One is trapped by what one cannot face.

Yet, as Baldwin says admiringly about Bessie Smith, the artist can escape all "definitions by becoming herself. This is still the only way to become a man or a woman—or an artist." If the artist must tell the truth at all costs, then no one tells the truth more chillingly than Baldwin. It is an item of faith with him that white Americans are "certainly the most dangerous people, of any color, to be found in the world today." In light of this threat to their mental and physical survival—which seems only superficially mitigated since slavery— black Americans have been forced to understand whites even better than whites understand themselves. The condition of the—normally silenced—outcasts of society often reflects badly on the psyches of the oppressors: "One can measure very neatly the white man's distance from his conscience—from himself—by observing the distance between white America and black America." Baldwin feels a double entitlement, as writer and as black, to utter the unpalatable truth about the latest phase of what he calls the "black diaspora": "The color of my skin . . . seems to operate as a most disagreeable mirror, and a great deal of one's energy is expended in reassuring white Americans that they do not see what they see."

Baldwin's confessions accuse us in the hope that we will eventually reform ourselves: "in the heart of the absolutely necessary accusation there is contained a plea." The positive side of Baldwin's prophecy is his vision of what America could be if it lived up to its full promise: "The liberation of Americans from the racial anguish which has crippled us for so long can only mean, truly, the creation of a new people in this still-new world." Even in accusation, blacks speak "out of the most passionate love, hoping to make the kingdom new, to make it honorable and worthy of life.' He still believes in the possibility of interracial community—"our endless connection with, and responsibility for each other"—but finds at present the idea of community only "among the submerged, the 'lowly': the Native American, the Mexican, the Puerto Rican, the Black."

Baldwin is one of the last remaining American writers with a vision of what it might mean, individually and societally, to be whole: In an era of fragmentation and compartmentalization, that's saying quite a lot. Yet time is running out: one prophecy of these essays that grows more sinister as the years pass: "If we do not now dare everything, the fulfillment of that prophecy . . . is upon us: *God gave Noah the rainbow sign, No more water, the fire next time!*"

The Price of the Ticket remains, thankfully, incomplete: There are more essays to come. Baldwin's latest work, *The Evidence of Things Not Seen*, continues to challenge our most treasured sureties—here in a lengthy meditation on the Atlanta child murder case. The book begins with a prophecy of doom borrowed from William Blake (which Baldwin first used in 1964 in "Words of a Native Son"): "A dog starv'd at his master's grave/Predicts the ruin of the state." Returning to Atlanta 26 years after his first major essay about Atlanta, "Nobody Knows My Name" (1959), Baldwin once more assesses the health of the American State. The mayor and most of the investigators may be black, but Atlanta, and the racist assumptions of Southern justice, have changed little, despite the contrary "evidence."

For Baldwin, the investigation culminates in "an unlikely and untidy murder case—or, more precisely, an unlikely case and an untidy trial." Williams was trapped by the kind of threadbare evidence (this case, literally "fibers") which white Southern justice once used to hang blacks from very thick ropes. Williams, convicted of committing two out of twenty-eight murders, shows a "pattern" that connects him to the other cases, but finally "it is impossible to claim that his guilt has been proven, any more than it can be proven that the murders have ceased." The entire notion of "pattern" upon which the district attorney's case against Williams hinged employs the same brand of self-legitimating semantics as, say, the notion of "Negro behavior."

Deplorably, the Williams conviction has the effect—if not the provable intent—of derailing further conversation about racial hatred and injustice in America. Atlanta becomes "the city too busy (making money) to hate" but also to witness the crimes that have taken place. In the end, whatever the true identity of their victimizers, the victims remain the same in 1985 as in 1959: "The only pattern I notice is that the victims were young Black males living in the purgatory of poverty."

Baldwin suffers from a few stylistic lapses during the essay: One senses that several all too painful issues—the intimation of black self-hatred; the unspoken subtleties of the New Racism of the eighties; the "homosexuality" issue; the amorphous nature of the case itself—blunted Baldwin's attack here, and kept him from getting to the deeper psychological truth of the events involved. But Baldwin's moral challenge to us has never been keener. In the closing paragraphs, Baldwin sees, with St. Paul, "the evidence of things unseen" which is "faith" in the ability of white society to change: "This is the only nation in the world that can hope to liberate—to begin to liberate—mankind." The prophet glimpses in the "evidence" of the present the unseen future: "I will not live to see anything resembling this hope come to pass. Yet I know that I *have* seen it—in fire and blood and anguish, true, but I have seen it." Reading Baldwin, one can almost see it too. The consistency of Baldwin's witness is impressive, but the intransigence of his listeners, and of racial oppression in general, remains troubling.

Chronology

1924   August 2: James Arthur (Baldwin) is born in Harlem, son of Emma Berdis Jones.

1927   Emma Jones marries David Baldwin, a storefront church preacher who has recently moved to Harlem from New Orleans.

1930-38   Attends P.S. 24 and Frederick Douglass Junior High School. Edits high school newspaper and studies with Countee Cullen, the advisor of the school literary club.

1938-42   Attends De Witt Clinton High School where he publishes stories in the school newspaper, *The Magpie*, which he and Richard Avedon edit.

1942   Upon graduation, Baldwin joins Emile Gapouya, a classmate, to become a railroad worker in Belle Mead, New Jersey.

1943   His father dies, August 1.

1944   Takes up residence in Greenwich Village and is introduced to Richard Wright. Begins to write a novel.

1945   Receives Eugene Saxton Fellowship, having been recommended by Richard Wright.

1946   Writes book reviews for *The Nation* and *The New Leader*.

1948   Awarded Rosenwald Fellowship. His first essay and short story are published, both in *Commentary*. Lives in Paris.

1953   *Go Tell It on the Mountain* is published.

1954   *The Amen Corner* is published. Baldwin receives a Guggenheim Fellowship.

1955   *Notes of a Native Son* is published. *The Amen Corner* performed at Howard University.

1956   *Giovanni's Room* is published; Baldwin receives a *Partisan Review* Fellowship and the National Institute of Arts and Letters Award.

1959   Receives Ford Foundation Grant.

1961   *Nobody Knows My Name* is published; the essay collection becomes a best-seller and receives a certificate of recognition from the National Conference on Christians and Jews.

1962   The best-selling *Another Country* is published as Baldwin travels to Africa.

1963   *The Fire Next Time* is published. Baldwin awarded the George Polk Memorial Award for magazine reporting.

1964   *Blues for Mr. Charlie* opens on Broadway, April 23, at the ANTA Theater, directed by Burgess Meredith. *Nothing Personal*, with photographs by Richard Avedon, is published.

1965   *The Amen Corner* is produced on Broadway. *Going to Meet the Man* is published.

1968   *Tell Me How Long the Train's Been Gone* is published.

1971   *A Rap on Race*, with Margaret Mead, is published.

1972   *No Name in the Street* and *One Day, When I Was Lost* are published.

1973   *A Dialogue*, with Nikki Giovanni, is published.

1974   *If Beale Street Could Talk* is published.

1976   *The Devil Finds Work* and *Little Man, Little Man* (a children's book) are published.

1979   *Just Above My Head* is published.

1980   In April, Baldwin signs with McGraw-Hill for more than $350,000 for rights to a forthcoming book, *Remember This House*. (All sixteen of his previous books were published by Dial Press.)

1982   Receives honorary degree from City University of New York.

1985   PBS television adaptation of *Go Tell It on the Mountain* is aired in January. *The Price of the Ticket: Collected Nonfiction 1948–1985* and *The Evidence of Things Not Seen* are published.

Contributors

HAROLD BLOOM, Sterling Professor of the Humanities at Yale University, is the author of *The Anxiety of Influence, Poetry and Repression*, and many other volumes of literary criticism. His forthcoming study, *Freud: Transference and Authority*, attempts a full-scale reading of all of Freud's major writings. A MacArthur Prize Fellow, he is general editor of five series of literary criticism published by Chelsea House.

F. W. DUPEE was Professor of English at Columbia University and the author of *Henry James* and *"The King of Cats" and Other Remarks on Writers and Writing*.

MARCUS KLEIN, Professor of English at the State University of New York at Buffalo, is the author of *After Alienation: American Novels in Mid-Century* and *Foreigners: The Making of American Literature, 1900–1940*.

PHILIP ROTH is a novelist whose books include *Portnoy's Complaint, Letting Go, The Professor of Desire, When She Was Good, The Ghost Writer, Zuckerman Unbound*, and *The Anatomy Lesson*.

CHARLES NEWMAN is the author of *A Child's History of America, New Axis or the "Little Ed" Stories, There Must Be More to Love Than Death: Three Short Novels*, and *White Jazz*.

EDWARD MARGOLIES is Professor of English at the College of Staten Island, City University of New York. He is the author of *The Art of Richard Wright* and *Native Sons: A Critical Study of Twentieth-Century Negro American Authors*.

ROGER ROSENBLATT is the author of *Black Fiction* and *Children of War*.

MARION BERGHAHN is the author of *Images of Africa in Black American Literature*.

PEARL K. BELL writes regularly on fiction for *Commentary* magazine.

C. W. E. BIGSBY is Reader in American Literature in the School of English and American Studies at the University of East Anglia in Norwich. He is the author of *Albee, Confrontation and Commitment: A Study of Contemporary American Drama, 1959–1966, A Critical Introduction to Twentieth Century American Drama: 1900–1940, Dada and Surrealism, Joe Orton, Tom Stoppard,* and *The Second Black Renaissance: Essays in Black Literature*.

STEPHEN ADAMS is the author of *The Homosexual as Hero in Contemporary Fiction* and *James Purdy*.

JAMES A. SNEAD is Professor of English and Comparative Literature at Yale University, and the author of the forthcoming *Figures of Division: William Faulkner's Major Novels*.

Bibliography

Allen, Shirley S. "Religious Symbolism and Psychic Reality in Baldwin's *Go Tell It on the Mountain*." *CLA Journal* 19 (1975): 173–99.

Baker, Houston A., Jr. *Long Black Song: Essays in Black American Literature and Culture.* Charlottesville: The University Press of Virginia, 1972.

Barksdale, Richard K. "Temple of the Fire Baptized." *Phylon* 14 (1953): 326–27.

Barrett, William. "Weight of the City." *Atlantic Monthly* (July 1962): 110–11.

Bell, George E. "The Dilemma of Love in *Go Tell It on the Mountain* and *Giovanni's Room*." *CLA Journal* 17 (1974): 397–406.

Bigsby, C. W. E. "The Committed Writer: James Baldwin as Dramatist." *Twentieth Century Literature* 13 (1967): 39–48.

Bone, Robert A. "The Novels of James Baldwin." *Triquarterly* 2 (Winter 1965): 3–20.

Breit, Harvey. "James Baldwin and Two Footnotes." In *The Creative Present: Notes on Contemporary American Fiction*, edited by Nona Balakian and Charles Simmons, 5–24. Garden City, N.Y.: Doubleday, 1963.

Brustein, Robert. "Everybody's Protest Play." *New Republic* (May 16, 1964): 35–37.

Bryant, Jerry H. "Wright, Ellison, Baldwin—Exorcising the Demon." *Phylon* 37 (1976): 174–88.

Burgess, Anthony. "The Postwar American Novel: A View from the Periphery." *American Scholar* 35 (Winter 1965–66): 150–56.

Burks, Mary Fair. "James Baldwin's Protest Novel: *If Beale Street Could Talk*." *Negro American Literature Forum* 10 (1976): 83–87.

Charney, Maurice. "James Baldwin's Quarrel with Richard Wright." *American Quarterly* 15 (1963): 63–75.

Cleaver, Eldridge. "Notes on a Native Son." *Ramparts* (June 1966): 51–56.

Clurman, Harold. "*Blues for Mister Charlie*." *The Nation* (May 1, 1964): 495–96.

———. "*The Amen Corner*." *The Nation* (May 10, 1964): 514–15.

Coles, Robert. "Baldwin's Burden." *Partisan Review* 31 (Summer 1964): 409–16.

———. "James Baldwin Back Home." *The New York Times Book Review* (July 31, 1977): 1, 22–24.

Cox, C. B., and A. R. Jones. "After the Tranquilized Fifties: Notes on Sylvia Plath and James Baldwin." *Critical Quarterly* 6 (1964): 107–22.

Curley, Thomas F. "The Quarrel with Time in American Fiction." *American Scholar* 29 (Autumn 1960): 552–60.

Daniels, Mark R. "Estrangement, Betrayal and Atonement: The Political Theory of James Baldwin." *Studies in Black Literature* 7 (Autumn 1976): 10–13.

Davenport, Guy. "Magic Realism in Prose." *National Review* (August 28, 1962): 153–54.

Davis, Arthur P. *From the Dark Tower: Afro-American Writers, 1900 to 1960.* Washington, D.C.: Howard University Press, 1974.

Davis, Charles T. "The Heavenly Voice of the Black American." In *Anagogic Qualities in Literature*, edited by Joseph P. Strelka, 107–19. University Park: Pennsylvania State University Press, 1971.

DeMott, Benjamin. "James Baldwin on the Sixties: Acts and Revelations." *Saturday Review* (May 27, 1972): 63–66.

Dickstein, Morris. "The Black Aesthetic in White America." *Partisan Review* 38 (1971): 376–95.

Eckman, Fern Marja. *The Furious Passage of James Baldwin.* New York: M. Evans and Company, 1966.

Ellison, Ralph. "Ralph Ellison Talks About James Baldwin." *Negro Digest* (September 1962): 61.

———. "Society, Morality, and the Novel." In *The Living Novel*, edited by Granville Hicks. New York: Macmillan, 1957.

Emanuel, James A., and Theodore L. Gross, eds. *Dark Symphony: Negro Literature in America*, 296–300, 588–89. New York: Free Press, 1968.

Fiedler, Leslie. "Caliban or Hamlet: An American Paradox." *Encounter* (April 1966): 23–27.

Finn, James. "The Identity of James Baldwin." *Commonweal* (October 26, 1962): 113–16.

Ford, Nick Aaron. *Black Insights: Significant Literature by Black Americans—1760 to the Present*, 192–219, 300–301. Waltham, Mass.: Ginn and Company, 1971.

Foster, David E. " 'Cause My House Fell Down': The Theme of the Fall in Baldwin's Novels." *Critique* 13, no. 2 (1971): 50–62.

Gayle, Addison, Jr. "A Defense of James Baldwin." *CLA Journal* 10 (1967): 201–8.

———. *The Way of the New World: The Black Novel in America.* Garden City, N. Y.: Doubleday, 1975.

Gilman, Richard. "News from the Novel." *New Republic* (August 17, 1968): 27–36.

Goodman, Paul. "Not Enough of a World to Grow In." *The New York Times Book Review* (June 24, 1962): 5.

Gross, Barry. "The 'Uninhabitable Darkness' of Baldwin's *Another Country*: Image and Theme." *Negro American Literature Forum* 6 (1972): 113–21.

Gross, Theodore L. *The Heroic Ideal in American Literature*, 166–79. New York: Free Press, 1971.

Harper, Howard M., Jr. *Desperate Faith: A Study of Bellow, Salinger, Mailer, Baldwin, and Updike*, 137–61. Chapel Hill: University of North Carolina Press, 1967.

Hemenway, Robert, ed. *The Black Novelist*, 111–33, 218–26. Columbus: Charles E. Merrill Publishing Company, 1970.

Hoffman, Stanton. "The Cities of Night: John Rechy's *City of Night* and the American Literature of Homosexuality." *Chicago Review* 17, nos. 2 and 3 (1964): 195–206.

Howe, Irving. "Black Boys and Native Sons." *Dissent* 10 (1963): 353–68.

Hughes, Langston. "From Harlem to Paris." *The New York Times* (February 26, 1956): 26.

Inge, M. Thomas. "James Baldwin's Blues." *Notes on Contemporary Literature* 24 (1972): 8–11.

Ivy, James W. "The Fairie Queen: Review of *Giovanni's Room*." *Crisis* 64 (February 1957): 123.

Jacobson, Dan. "James Baldwin as Spokesman." *Commentary* 32 (1961): 497–502.

Kent, George E. *Blackness and the Adventure of Western Culture*. Chicago: Third World Press, 1972.

Kim, Kichung. "Wright, the Protest Novel, and Baldwin's Faith." *CLA Journal* 17 (1974): 387–96.

Kinnamon, Kenneth, ed. *James Baldwin: A Collection of Critical Essays*. Englewood Cliffs, N. J.: Prentice-Hall, 1974.

Lee, Brian. "James Baldwin: Caliban to Prospero." In *The Black American Writer*, edited by C. W. E. Bigsby, vol. 1, 169–79. Deland, Fla.: Everett/Edwards, 1969.

Levin, David. "Baldwin's Autobiographical Essays: The Problem of Negro Identity." *Massachusetts Review* 5 (1964): 239–47.

Macdonald, Dwight. "The Bright Young Man in the Arts." *Esquire* (September 1958): 38–40.

Macebuh, Stanley. *James Baldwin: A Critical Study*. New York: Third Press, 1973.

MacInnes, Colin. "Dark Angel: The Writings of James Baldwin." *Encounter* 21 (August 1963): 22–33.

Marcus, Stephen. "The American Negro in Search of Identity." *Commentary* 16 (1953): 456–63.

McCluskey, John. " 'If Beale Street Could Talk.' " *Black World* 24 (December 1974): 51–52, 88–91.

Mellard, James M. "Racism, Formula, and Popular Fiction." *Journal of Popular Culture* 5, no. 1 (Summer 1971): 10–37.

Merton, Thomas. "The Negro Revolt." *Jubilee* (September 1963): 39–43.

Meserve, Walter. "James Baldwin's 'Agony Way.' " In *The Black American Writer*, edited by C. W. E. Bigsby, vol. 2, 171–86. Deland, Fla.: Everett/Edwards, 1969.

Moller, Karin. *The Theme of Identity in the Essays of James Baldwin: An Interpretation*. Gothenburg Studies in English Series, 32. Atlantic Highlands, N. J.: Humanities Press, 1975.

Neal, Lawrence P. "The Black Writers' Role: James Baldwin." *Liberator* 6 (April 1966): 10–11.

Noble, David W. *The Eternal Adam and the New World Garden: The Central Myth in the American Novel Since 1830*. New York: George Braziller, 1968.

O'Brien, Conor Cruise. "White Gods and Black Americans." *New Statesman* (May 1, 1964): 681–82.

O'Daniel, Therman B. "James Baldwin: An Interpretive Study." *CLA Journal* 7 (September 1963): 37–47.

———, ed. *James Baldwin: A Critical Evaluation*. Washington, D.C.: Howard University Press, 1977.

Patterson, H. Orlando. "The Essays of James Baldwin." *New Left Review* 26 (Summer 1964): 31–38.

Podhoretz, Norman. *Doings and Undoings*. New York: Farrar, Straus, and Company, 1964.

Pratt, Louis H. "James Baldwin and 'The Literary Ghetto.' " *CLA Journal* 20 (1976): 262–72.

Redding, Saunders. "The Problems of the Negro Writer." *Massachusetts Review* 6 (Autumn–Winter 1964–65): 57–70.

Sayre, Robert F. "James Baldwin's Other Country." In *Contemporary American Novelists*, edited by Harry T. Moore, 158–69. Carbondale: Southern Illinois University Press, 1964.

Scott, Nathan A., Jr. "Judgment Marked by a Cellar: The American Negro Writer and the Dialectic of Despair." *The Denver Quarterly* 2 (Summer 1967): 5–35.

Simmons, Harvey G. "James Baldwin and the Negro Conundrum." *Antioch Review* 23 (1963): 250–60.

Spender, Stephen. "James Baldwin: Voice of a Revolution." *Partisan Review* 30 (1963): 256–60.

Strandley, Fred L. "James Baldwin: The Crucial Situation." *South Atlantic Quarterly* 65 (1966): 371–81.

————. "*Another Country*, Another Time." *Studies in the Novel* 4 (1972): 504–12.

Wade, Melvin, and Margaret Wade. "The Black Aesthetic in the Black Novel." *Journal of Black Studies* 2 (June 1972): 391–408.

Watson, Edward A. "The Novels of James Baldwin: Case-Book of a 'Lover's War' with the United States." *Queen's Quarterly* 72, no. 2 (Summer 1965): 385–402.

Weatherby, W. J. *Squaring Off: Mailer vs. Baldwin*. New York: Mason/Charter, 1977.

West, Anthony. "Sorry Lives." *New Yorker* (June 20, 1953): 85.

Acknowledgments

"James Baldwin and 'The Man' " by F. W. Dupee from *"The King of the Cats" and Other Remarks on Writers and Writing*, 2d ed. by F. W. Dupee, © 1971 by the Estate of F. W. Dupee. Reprinted by permission of The University of Chicago Press.

"A Question of Identity" (originally entitled "James Baldwin: A Question of Identity") by Marcus Klein from *After Alienation: American Novels in Mid-Century*, by Marcus Klein, © 1962, 1964 by The World Publishing Co. Reprinted by permission of New York Books for Libraries Press.

"*Blues for Mr. Charlie*" (originally entitled "Channel X: Two Plays on the Race Conflict") by Philip Roth from *The New York Review of Books* 2, no. 8 (May 28, 1964), © 1964 by The New York Review, Inc. Reprinted by permission.

"The Lesson of the Master: Henry James and James Baldwin" by Charles Newman from *The Yale Review* 56, no. 1 (October 1966), © 1966 by Yale University. Reprinted by permission.

"The Negro Church: James Baldwin and the Christian Vision" by Edward Margolies from *Native Sons: A Critical Study of Twentieth-Century Black American Authors*, © 1968 by Edward Margolies. Reprinted by permission of J. B. Lippincott Co.

"Out of Control: *Go Tell It on the Mountain* and *Another Country*" (originally entitled "Lord of the Rings" and "White Outside") by Roger Rosenblatt from *Black Fiction*, by Roger Rosenblatt, © 1974 by the President and Fellows of Harvard College. Reprinted by permission of Harvard University Press.

"Images of Africa in the Writings of James Baldwin" (originally entitled "The Transitional Phase – Time of Scepticism") by Marion Berghahn from *Images of Africa in Black American Literature*, by Marion Berghahn ©1977 by Marion Berghahn. Reprinted by permission of Rowman and Littlefield and the Macmillan Press, London and Basingstoke.

"Coming Home" (originally entitled "Roth & Baldwin: Coming Home") by Pearl K. Bell from *Commentary* 68, no. 6 (December 1979), © 1979 by the American Jewish Committee. Reprinted by permission; all rights reserved.

"The Divided Mind of James Baldwin" by C. W. E. Bigsby from *Journal of American Studies* 13, no. 3 (December 1979), © 1979 by Cambridge University Press. Reprinted by permission.

"*Giovanni's Room*: The Homosexual as Hero" (originally entitled "James Baldwin") by Stephen Adams from *The Homosexual as Hero in Contemporary Fiction by Stephen Adams*, © 1980 by Stephen Adams. Reprinted by permission of Vision Press Limited.

"Baldwin Looks Back" by James A. Snead from *Los Angeles Times* (December 1, 1985), © 1985 by The Times–Mirror Co. Reprinted by permission.

Index